NICK BAKER'S
BUG ZOO

A Dorling Kindersley book

DK

LONDON, NEW YORK,
MELBOURNE, MUNICH, and DELHI

Senior editor Ben Morgan
Senior designer Sadie Thomas
Designers Gabriela Rosecka, Lauren Rosier
Additional editing by Wendy Horobin
Photography Will Heap
Picture researcher Rob Nunn
Illustrations Laurie Peters
Production editor Clare McLean
Creative director Jane Bull
Category publisher Mary Ling

First published in Great Britain in 2010 by
Dorling Kindersley Limited, 80 Strand, London WC2R 0RL

A CIP catalogue record for this book
is available from the British Library
ISBN 978-1-40535-348-9
Colour reproduction by MDP, UK
Printed and bound by
Toppan, China

Discover more at
www.dk.com

WHO IS THIS?

CONTENTS

Do you know what I eat?

Welcome to Bug Zoo!!

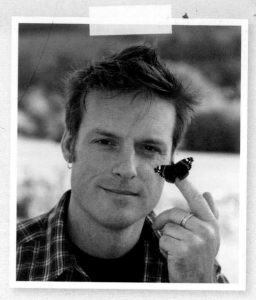

Why start a bug zoo? Well, why not? Just because bugs are everywhere doesn't mean they're any less interesting than the animals you might see in a real zoo. In fact, the chances are that you know more about the exotic animals in a zoo than you do about the tiny creatures living right under your nose.

When I was growing up, my parents wouldn't let me keep animals in the house and I can't say I blame them. It didn't help my cause when my stick insects got out and defoliated my mum's houseplants or when I forgot to put the lid back on my ant city... But such mishaps didn't hold me back. We had an old shed and I quickly purloined it for my collection. Armed with a curious mind and a few jars, **I built my first bug zoo**, and wow, did it open my eyes!

Each pot, pickle jar, and matchbox was a source of wonder, a dramatic little world with as much excitement as any TV soap opera. I witnessed what looked like scenes from a science fiction film – some so terrifyingly bizarre they'd be unfit for broadcast. I saw MURDER and *cannibalism*, slashing blades and chemical warfare. I watched caterpillars being reincarnated as butterflies. And I learnt first-hand that **there's nothing ladylike about a ladybird!**

Starting a bug zoo is the perfect way to immerse yourself in the alien world of bugs. When you get down to their level (and that means getting *really* close – eye to compound eye, finger to feeler), it puts a fresh spin on the way you see things: a lawn becomes an exotic savannah, a hedge becomes a jungle, a garden pond becomes as mysterious as the deep sea. You don't even need to use your imagination – there are unexplored worlds right on your doorstep, and the fantastical animals are real. You just have to open your eyes.

Building a zoo means you can become an explorer, a hunter, a collector of fine zoological specimens and, of course, a zoo keeper. You don't need much to get started – just a table and a few jars will do. And you can capture your exhibits anywhere. Tune into their world and I can promise you this: you will never, ever be bored again.

Happy hunting!

Nick Baker

I proudly dedicate this book to my own little bug hunter, Elvie. Whose very first word was "moth"!

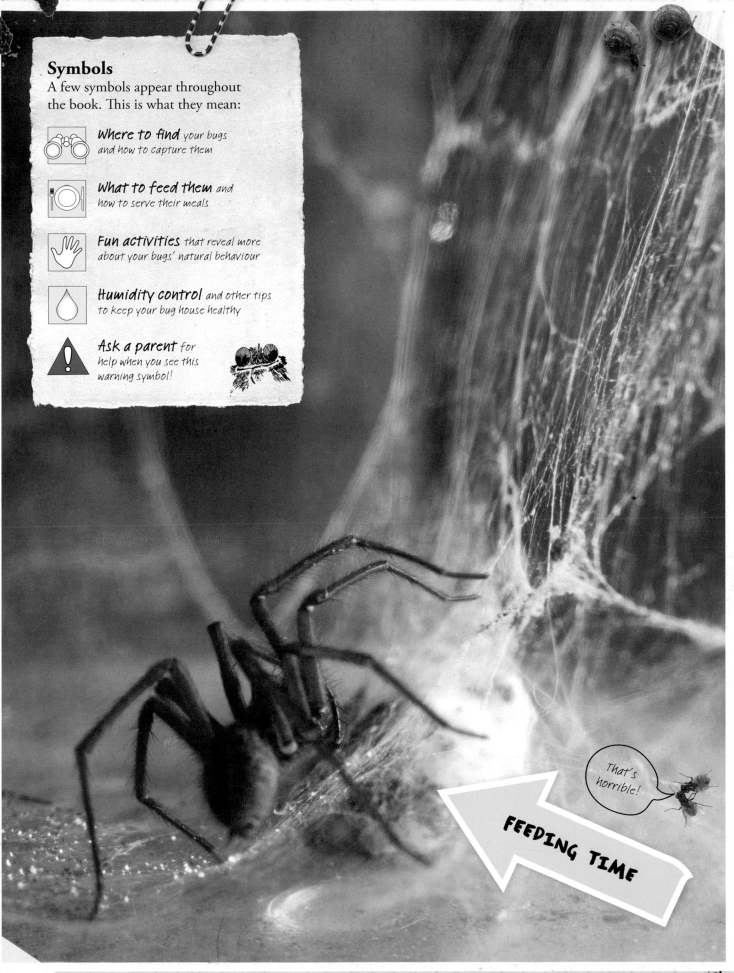

Symbols

A few symbols appear throughout the book. This is what they mean:

Where to find your bugs and how to capture them

What to feed them and how to serve their meals

Fun activities that reveal more about your bugs' natural behaviour

Humidity control and other tips to keep your bug house healthy

Ask a parent for help when you see this warning symbol!

That's horrible!

FEEDING TIME

ZOO TOOLS

All zoo keepers need equipment to manage their collections, whether it's a broom and shovel to muck out the monkeys or special tongs to move snakes around. The same applies to your bug zoo, so having the right bits of kit to hand will make day-to-day bug maintenance just that little bit easier. The good news is that most of the things you need can be found around the house without you having to raid the piggy bank.

Kitchen towel

I love this stuff and use it to carpet insect containers, to wipe up spilt gunk, to block vases (which stops insects drowning), and to provide a source of moisture.

Paintbrush

Even the gentlest of fingers can squash a bug. For delicate jobs, a fine-haired paintbrush is essential. Use it to pick up pseudoscorpions, nudge caterpillars along, or even to brush out frass (insect poo) from awkward corners.

Notebook

It's a good idea to keep a notebook recording what goes on in the lives of your specimens. You can measure their growth and keep tabs on when they moult, mate, and feed. If you see any interesting behaviour, jot it down – you may be the first person to witness it!

Tweezers (forceps)

These are a delicate extension of your own thumb and forefinger. While it's not a good idea to use them to handle bugs directly, they are useful for picking up other small items. You can make them more bug-friendly by gluing small foam pads to the ends!

Scissors

Useful for trimming kitchen towel and snipping sprigs off plants.

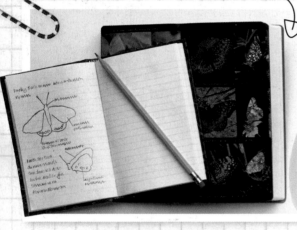

You can add sketches or photos to your notebook. Remember that many digital cameras have excellent "macro" lenses for taking close-ups.

You can make tweezers from wooden kebab skewers and an elastic band. Wind the band around one stick to form a hinge. Then wind the rest around both sticks.

Spoon

Ideal for scooping up everything from water creatures to ladybirds. When used in conjunction with a paintbrush, you have a miniature dustpan and brush!

Sieve or tea strainer

These are cheap and make excellent nets. The sieve is a great tool for pond dipping and can be taped to a garden cane for an instant pond net. The tea strainer is ideal for more delicate tasks, such as transferring creatures from tank to tank.

Mist sprayer
A regular spray with warm water will keep things nice and humid in your bug houses.

Labels
Make labels for your containers. Write down the type and number of bugs inside the container and the date you caught them.

Cardboard
Cardboard or black paper makes the perfect blind or privacy curtain.

Pencils
I prefer pencils to pens for making notes because if you spill water on your writing or it gets damp, you can still read it.

Netting
Netting (or old tights) can be used to make ventilation panels in insect cages, nets to capture bugs, or lids for jars, secured with an elastic band. Use **black netting** if you possibly can – it's much easier to see through.

Magnifying lens
Probably one of the most useful bits of kit any bug zoo owner can have. Most of the creatures in your collection are small, so anything that magnifies their lives will make studying them just that little bit more fun! Magnifications of 8x or 10x are perfect. Get the best one you can afford and keep it handy on a string around your neck.

Plastic lids
The lids of milk cartons and other containers make great food or water bowls.

Elastic bands
Useful for holding scraps of netting in place over the necks of jars.

USB microscope
Lets bring things up to date! These are not essential, but if you have a computer, a USB microscope will allow you to view small bugs in amazing detail. Most give you the option of recording still or moving images, and some magnify up to 200 times! A bendy stand helps give a steady image if you use high magnifications.

Glue
PVA or similar glue is useful for securing objects to the sides of containers and is not toxic to bugs that might unwittingly nibble it.

Tape
Masking tape is useful for sticking covers onto enclosures to create private and dark spaces for your captives.

CATCHING AND KEEPING

You don't need specialist containers for catching and keeping bugs. With a bit of trial and error, you'll soon discover how to adapt household containers for all your zoological needs, whether they're jars or boxes that once housed jam, sweets, chocolates, or shoes. The secret to creating a good habitat is to match the container to the animal and to make sure each type of bug gets just the right balance of moisture, ventilation, and temperature.

Making a pooter

It's a serious bit of kit with a silly name. A pooter is simply a suction device that allows you to collect very small creatures that would otherwise be maddeningly fiddly to pick up. You can buy professional pooters but it's easy to make one out of common household items.

COLLECTING CAPTIVES

1. *Ask an adult* to make two holes in the plastic lid of a spice or herb jar. An easy way to use this is to heat a metal skewer and use it to melt the plastic.

2. *Cut two lengths* of plastic tube, 30 cm (12 in) and 20 cm (8 in) long. Push the ends of each through the holes in the plastic lid. They should fit snugly.

Using the pooter

It's a good idea to practice with the pooter. Try sucking up grains of rice or rolled up bits of paper. Put the short tube in your mouth, position the end of the long tube over the dummy bug, and then give a short, sharp suck.

When trying it on live creatures, make sure you only use it on animals that will fit easily through the tube. Don't suck up slimy creatures or those with long legs or delicate wings that could get damaged. Oh, and one last tip: don't suck on the wrong tube, especially if you've already got insects in the pooter. It's not nice for you or them if you end up getting a mouthful of bugs!

3. *Wrap cloth* around the internal end of shorter tube and secure it with an elastic band. This is the tube you will suck through.

4. *Put coloured tape* around the same tube. This is to remind you which tube to put in your mouth, which is critical, as you'll see later!

8

The more you get into keeping and studying bugs, the more you'll become a connoisseur of containers!

Small plastic pots from deli tubs to glitter tubes are ideal for transporting bugs or housing small species. You can also buy purpose-made containers from biological suppliers.

Animal tanks from pet shops can serve as either aquariums or terrariums (dry habitats). As small animals and moisture can escape through the slotted lid, you may need to put netting or a sheet of plastic under it.

Shoeboxes and plastic tubs make good insect houses if you cut out a window and replace it with a see-through screen of black netting. See page 25.

Glass aquariums give better visibility than plastic as the glass does not scratch easily. See page 57 to find out how to create a freshwater habitat in an aquarium.

A homemade wormery is easy to make from wood, perspex, and bulldog clips. Instructions on page 30.

Round tins can be adapted to make superb houses for larger insects. See page 48.

9

WOODLICE

Go into your garden now and lift something up – a rock, a log, a flowerpot, anything. It doesn't really matter, because you can bet that under each one will be a herd of what look like miniature armadillos: woodlice. Despite their familiarity, there is a lot more to woodlice than meets the eye, and they make a very interesting addition to your invertebrate zoo.

Brood pouch
The woodlouse has a lovely boat-shaped body, albeit upside down. Females use the ample storage space to keep eggs in a fluid-filled "brood pouch". This usually contains about 50 eggs but can hold as many as 260. The eggs hatch a month or two after mating and the youngsters then spend another week inside the pouch before being released.

CREATURE FEATURES

Exoskeleton
Woodlice must shed their external skeleton in order to grow. Unlike insects, they moult in two stages. First they take off their "trousers" by moulting the back half; then they moult the front half and go "topless". The old skin is eaten and recycled.

Moulted skin

New skin

Front half ready to moult

ANTENNA

ARMOUR PLATE

EYE

Legs
Count the legs. Woodlice have 14 and so are neither insects nor arachnids. They are actually crustaceans – close relatives of sea creatures like crabs and lobsters. While most crustaceans live in water, woodlice live on land but prefer damp places because they breathe through gills.

14 LEGS

Woodlice have been known to live for FOUR years!

Woodlice are known by many different names, including pill bugs, sow bugs, bibble bugs, doodlebugs, buck

Close cousins

Woodlice belong to a branch of the crustacean family known as the isopods, the biggest of which are giant isopods up to 37 cm (15 in) long! These monsters are common in the sea. They trundle around on the sea floor scavenging on dead matter, just as woodlice do on land.

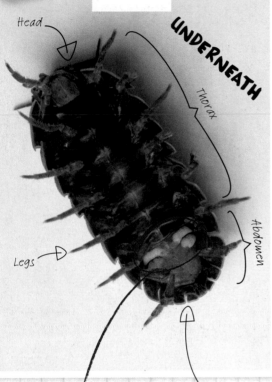

Head

UNDERNEATH

Thorax

Abdomen

Legs

Gills

Just like their aquatic relatives, woodlice breathe through gills. These need to be covered with a thin layer of water to work well, which is why woodlice need moisture. Some woodlice have developed lungs of sorts; these are seen as white patches on the gills. These white areas are riddled with air tubes that help the woodlouse get oxygen from the air.

Uropods

Most woodlice have a pair of small tails called uropods. Aquatic crustaceans like lobsters have large uropods that they flap to help them swim. The small uropods of woodlice are used to produce defensive chemicals and to soak up water.

Pill bugs can roll into a ball for protection.

who to keep

There are thousands of woodlouse species, but you're most likely to find one of the five species below. Native to Europe, these have been spread by people and are now found worldwide.

Common rough woodlouse
(*Porcellio scaber*)
The most common in my garden, it loves the drier places and is easily recognized by its grey matt appearance. Look at it through a magnifying glass and its surface is covered in tiny little pimples. Length 17 mm (0.7 in).

Common shiny woodlouse
(*Oniscus asellus*)
Probably the second most common species in gardens, it looks glossy on the surface and has tiny yellowish flecks. Max. length 16 mm (0.6 in).

Pill woodlouse
(*Armadillidium vulgare*)
This distinctive species has a smooth, glossy surface and an almost rounded or domed body. It's one of the few species that rolls into a ball when disturbed. Found in drier places than the others. Length 18 mm (0.7 in).

Striped woodlouse
(*Philoscia muscorum*)
This smaller species comes in a variety of different colours from brick red to yellow as well as brown and grey, but one thing they all have is a dark stripe along the back. Length 11 mm (0.4 in).

Common pygmy woodlouse
(*Trichoniscus pusillus*)
A tiddler with a top size of 5 mm (0.2 in). It's actually common but often overlooked because of its size. The best place to find it is among leaf litter in woodlands. It has clusters of tiny little black eyes (three on each side) and the ends of its antennae are very fine and hair-like.

gs, cheeselogs, chucky pigs, pisse-beds, coffin cutters, gamma sows, roly-polies, and cudworms.

Use a **plastic tub** to collect your captives.

THE LOUSE HOUSE

Woodlice are easy to keep. The key to creating a good louse house is to understand their basic requirements: they like it dark and a little damp – but not soggy. A plastic or glass tank or jar with a little soil in is all that's needed, and because woodlice like to hide from view you need to provide a nice, dark **hiding place.**

To trap woodlice, bore a hole in a potato and put it in the garden. Woodlice love dark, damp places and will soon crawl inside.

1. **To find lots of woodlice,** look under the bark of a rotten log or lift a rock and look underneath. If you go out at night with a torch you may well find woodlice roving about on walls, patios, and flowerbeds.

2. **Put a layer** of soil or all-purpose compost in the bottom of the tank. As well as providing food, this will help control humidity. If you want, add some "furniture" to your louse house to make it look interesting.

3. **Place a piece of bark** against the side of the tank for the woodlice to hide behind. Prop it up with stones or glue it in place with silicone sealant.

4. **To make the hiding** place dark, tape a flap of card on the outside of the tank to make a blackout curtain. Make sure you can lift it easily to spy on the woodlice.

LOUSE ENCLOSURE

Black curtain

To maintain a humid environment in your louse house, give the inside a couple of squirts with a mist-sprayer each week and put a wad of damp moss in the tank.

Woodlice have a rotten diet, quite literally. They eat dead stuff, mainly plant material such as WOOD (hence their name), leaves, and the droppings of plant-eating animals. For a bit of variety you can feed your woodlice bits of **carrot and potato** too.

Woodlouse droppings may build up, but don't clean them out – the woodlice will EAT them. The droppings consist of dry, powdered wood that has passed through the woodlouse's gut 90 per cent undigested and so makes for another good meal! The droppings are also important in the recycling process, turning wood into soft pellets of compost that a host of other organisms can digest.

Dysdera

Woodlice produce defensive chemicals that make them taste foul to most predators, but a few specialized animals can eat them, including shrews, toads, and the so-called woodlouse spiders (Dysdera).

Eeek, spider!!!

Tagging

One of the problems of dealing with animals that live in a colony is being able to identify and keep up with individuals. One solution is to use non-toxic permanent marker pens or paint to dab a very small coloured spot on top of each woodlouse. Make a record of who's who and note down what they get up to each day. Remember, though, that when a woodlouse sheds its skin it will shed its mark and its identity!

5. ADD YOUR CAPTIVES!

Bark

potato

6. After a day or so, the woodlice will have settled in and found the hiding place. Lift the blackout curtain to watch them, but don't keep it open too long or they'll see through your scheme and wander off looking for another dark place to hide.

SLUGS & SNAILS

Slugs and snails are almost universally hated by human beings thanks to the habits of the relatively few species that have a taste for garden plants. However, if you get to know these creatures well you'll discover a secret world that – although a little slimy – is filled with fascinating weirdness and surprisingly little to loathe.

Hairy snails

Slugs are essentially snails without shells. Having no shell means they can slip into tiny gaps and squirm into soil, but they are more prone to drying out.

Mantle

CREATURE FEATURES

Distant cousin!

Meet the family

Slugs and snails belong to a huge family of animals known as molluscs. The molluscs mostly live in water and include octopuses, squid, and all the creatures that live inside seashells. The shell dwellers come in two forms: those with a shell made of two halves, like clams, and those with a classic seaside seashell – the gastropods. Slugs and snails are gastropods too. The word gastropod means "belly foot", and if you watch how a snail "walks" you'll realize it's a truly excellent name.

SHELL
Most snail shells are "right-handed", meaning that the spiral curls clockwise (to the right) from the centre. But if you're lucky you might find a left-handed snail. These are very rare and are known as "snail kings".

THE TAIL
This is not really a true tail but the trailing edge of the foot.

The world's **largest** land snail is the giant African snail. One specimen grew to 39.3 cm (15.5 in) when fully extended!

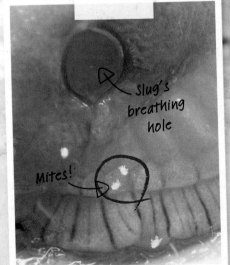

Slug's breathing hole

Mites!

BREATHING HOL
Slugs and snails breathe through a hole in the mantle. Look very closely at a slug's breathing hole and you might notice excitable white specks running in and out. These are mites that live on the slug's skin.

Growth ridges

A snail's shell is made of the mineral calcium carbonate (chalk), which snails get from their food. Look carefully at a shell and you'll see tiny ridges. These are growth rings that develop as growth slows down in winter and then speeds up again in spring.

Chalk

Use a torch to watch the eye shoot down the tentacle!

MANTLE

The materials that form a snail's shell are produced by a special part of the body wall called the mantle. When a snail retreats into its shell, it's the mantle you're left looking at. In slugs, the mantle is the thickened, leathery area on their back.

EYES

At the tips of the long tentacles are tiny eyes like black dots. These sense light and dark and can't see much else. Touch a snail's eye with your finger — it will shoot down the tentacle as the tentacle rolls in on itself like a pullover sleeve. Wait a moment and the tentacle will come back out as blood is pumped into it.

SHELL LIP

If the edge of the shell is thin and papery, the snail is still growing. If there's a nice, thick lip, the snail is fully grown.

TENTACLES

The four wiggly tentacles on the front are the snail's main sense organs. The long top pair contain eyes. The lower pair are sensitive to touch, taste, and smell.

very sensitive

THE FOOT

This is not a foot in the classic sense but a very muscular organ used to "surf" the carpet of slime that it lays down as it moves.

FOOT FRINGE

MOUTH

Slugs and snails scrape at leaves with a special kind of tongue called a radula, which is covered with tiny teeth.

Eye

MAKE A MOLLUSC MANSION

For tiny snail species, any clear-sided container is fine, but for larger species such as common garden snails, use a big jar or an old fish tank. Your snail house must have a SECURE LID that the snails can't push off. You'll also need to maintain a humid environment, but with enough ventilation to stop things getting mouldy and smelly.

Finding your captives

Go out on a warm, wet night and you'll find slugs and snails everywhere, but during the day nothing but a **silvery trail** can be seen. This is because these animals have thin skin and **lose water** easily in bright sun or wind. When the sun goes down, the humidity rises and they come out of hiding. To find them during the day, look under rocks and flowerpots, behind ivy, or in dark, damp crevices.

Maintenance of your "Gastropets" palace

Feeding

You'll soon realize how fussy slugs and snails can be – not all of them like our lettuces, despite what gardeners may think! Give your animals a choice and experiment with their diet. Try cucumber, tomatoes, bread, wild plants, dead leaves, grass cuttings, and dead wood. Put the food in small dishes to keep things tidy.

Climate control

If your snails stop moving, they may be too dry. In dry weather, snails can go into a form of hibernation known as "aestivation" and may even seal their shells shut with a waterproof skin. To keep humidity up, give them a quick spray of water once a day and reduce ventilation so the moisture doesn't evaporate too quickly.

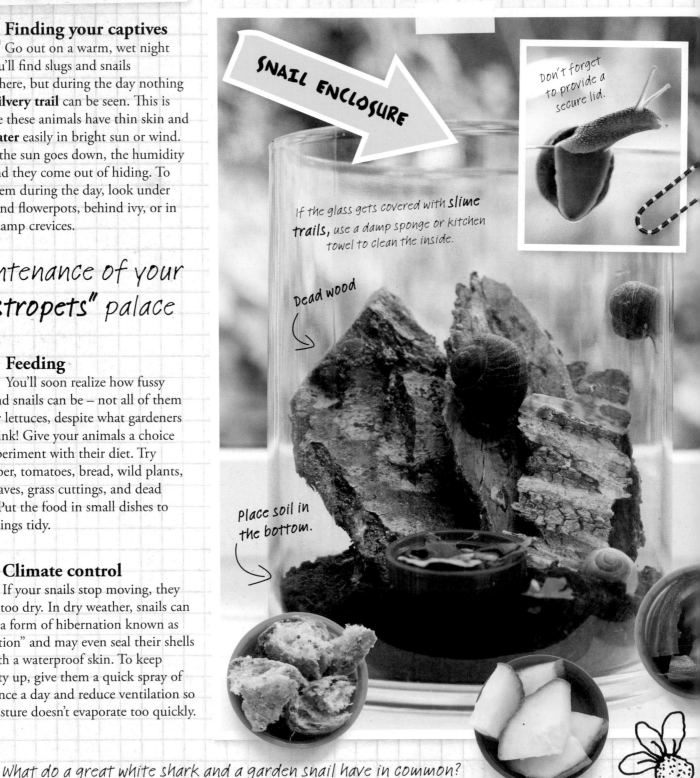

SNAIL ENCLOSURE

Don't forget to provide a secure lid.

If the glass gets covered with **slime trails,** use a damp sponge or kitchen towel to clean the inside.

Dead wood

Place soil in the bottom.

What do a great white shark and a garden snail have in common?

Look out for glass snails, which have transparent shells.

Tagging
To keep track of individuals, mark their shells with a permanent marker pen or spots of nail varnish. You can do the same with the snails in your garden. For instance, mark those behind the shed 1 to 10 in red and those under the ivy 1 to10 in yellow. Then go out at night with a torch and plot their positions on a map of your garden. How far do they wander? Do they return home?

Radula

Old timer
The owner of the snail above coloured it with purple nail varnish one year and pink the next and discovered that it stayed in the same garden for years.

Reveal the radula
To see your snail's mouth in action, make a soupy mixture from honey, water, and ground-up leaves and paint this on the inside of your mollusc house. Then wait for one of your molluscs to discover the treat (or place a snail on the glass). From outside you'll see the special tongue, or "radula", in action as your snail scrapes off the sugary mixture to satisfy its several thousand sweet teeth!

Banded snail

Mmm, I smell fresh bread!

It's said that a garden snail can smell food from 50 cm (20 in) away!

The smell test
Once you've discovered your snails' favourite food, why not **test their powers of smell?** First, give your snails an appetite by starving them for a couple of days. (Don't feel bad, in France they do this before cooking them – at least yours will have a happier ending.) Put the snails on a smooth table, place the food nearby, and watch. Move the food and see if the snails follow it. What's the maximum distance over which they respond?

Snails need a source of calcium for their shells. This is easy to supply in the form of a cuttlefish bone, which you can buy in a pet shop.

Meet the family

There are around 4500 aphid species, of which the most familiar are those that wash out of our salad: greenflies and blackflies (though neither are true flies and for most of the year they don't even have wings). The rest of the family come in all manner of colours, including pink, yellow, grey, mottled, and white. All of them feed by poking their mouthparts into plants and drinking the sap that flows out.

APHIDS...
THE HUNGRY HERDS

Also known as greenflies, aphids are plant-eating pests hated by gardeners the world over. I've included them in the book not only because they make great food for other species in your bug zoo, especially ladybirds, but because aphids are actually fascinating little animals in their own right. With a bit of help from a magnifying glass or microscope, you'll discover some of the weird tricks that make these little insects have such a BIG impact.

In perfect conditions, a single aphid can produce a family of BILLIONS in a single year!

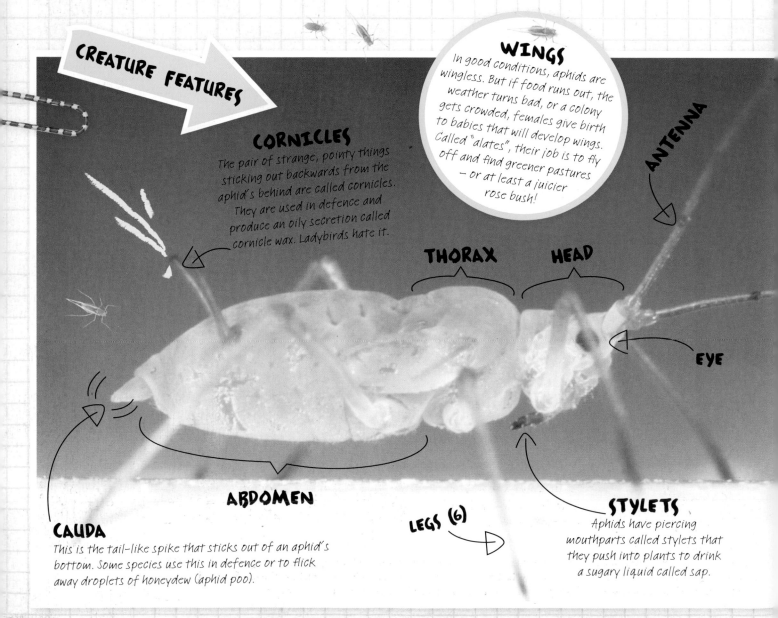

CREATURE FEATURES

CORNICLES
The pair of strange, pointy things sticking out backwards from the aphid's behind are called cornicles. They are used in defence and produce an oily secretion called cornicle wax. Ladybirds hate it.

WINGS
In good conditions, aphids are wingless. But if food runs out, the weather turns bad, or a colony gets crowded, females give birth to babies that will develop wings. Called "alates", their job is to fly off and find greener pastures – or at least a juicier rose bush!

THORAX

HEAD

ANTENNA

EYE

ABDOMEN

LEGS (6)

CAUDA
This is the tail-like spike that sticks out of an aphid's bottom. Some species use this in defence or to flick away droplets of honeydew (aphid poo).

STYLETS
Aphids have piercing mouthparts called stylets that they push into plants to drink a sugary liquid called sap.

Finding aphids

In spring and summer you'll find aphids on the leaves and stalks of sweet peas, beans, roses, thistles, stinging nettles, and maple (sycamore) trees. If you don't have these plants in your garden, plant broad beans or sweet peas in spring and the aphids will soon appear.

HOUSING THE HERD

You don't really need a "house" for your herd. All you need to keep aphids is a plant infested with them and a jar of water or vase. Use scissors to take a cutting and transfer it carefully to the jar. I say "carefully" because if you jolt the stem, the insects will drop off, thinking they're under attack by a giant predator. Keep the aphid jar in a sunny place – a windowsill is ideal.

Place the aphid jar on a black mat or black paper to collect moulted skins and droplets of sticky honeydew.

Sweet pea plant

Aphids

Keep the plant watered

MAINTAINING THE HERD

As your aphids multiply, they will take their toll on the plant they're all sucking on. To make sure they get enough food, add fresh cuttings to the jar. Aphids can be fussy feeders, so always use the same type of plant. Make sure the fresh stem touches the old one near the clusters of aphids so that the aphids will find it and move across.

Thinning out

You may need to thin out the numbers if things get crowded – otherwise the colony will start producing winged females that fly off to find new plants. Use a small paintbrush to tap unwanted aphids into a container. You can feed these to your ladybirds or release them back into the garden – an act that will probably mystify your parents!

Yum, dinner!

THE APHID'S SECRET WEAPON

Use a paintbrush to knock off every aphid except one.

Here's an experiment that will show you just why aphids are so successful. Simply take a cut stem with a few aphids on it and knock off all but the biggest and fattest one without wings. This is your foundress and she will be a female (they almost always are). Your job now is to make a note of the date and, each day, record the number of aphids on the plant. It won't be long before lots of babies appear...

Week 1

Week 2

Week 3

A female aphid lives about a month and has 3–8 babies a day. Now, in some species each of these is born *already pregnant* and can start giving birth a week later. In this way, a single female can give rise to billions of aphids in a year. If all the offspring of your foundress survived and gave birth themselves, you'd have enough insects after a year to make a line stretching more than four times around the Earth. That would require a lot of sweet peas! Fortunately this never happens as aphids are eaten by many other animals.

Virgin birth

The aphid's secret weapon is the ability to give birth without mating, a trick known as parthenogenesis. Quite a few insects do this and it lets them exploit a food supply quickly. To speed things up further, aphids give birth to live young rather than laying eggs, and, as we've seen, those babies are born pregnant – something scientists call "telescoping generations". It's a bit like Russian dolls, but with living insects.

What do bees make "forest honey" from?

Moulting

Like all insects, aphids have an external skeleton and must shed this from time to time so they can grow. Because there are a lot of aphids in your colony, there will nearly always be someone moulting. Watch how they split open their old skin and almost drop out upside down. Put a bit of black paper under the colony and watch the empty skins pile up.

Wings

Towards the end of the year, winged females and males appear. These mate and then disperse, the females either hibernating or laying eggs. Winged females may appear at other times if the colony gets overcrowded.

> Aphids plug their sharp stylets into a plant's veins and then sit back as the plant's sugary food supply is pumped right through their body. They don't even have to suck!

Do aphids have a sense of smell?

Watch how an aphid responds when you touch it gently but repeatedly with a fine-haired paintbrush. You might see a fluid come out of the ends of its cornicles. This waxy secretion is sticky and in some species contains foul-tasting chemicals and a scent known as an alarm pheromone. The scent warns other members of the herd that they're under attack.

> Quick, run!

Watch what happens if you get some of the waxy secretion on your paintbrush and waft it around. The other aphids will pull out their stylets and **drop off the plant** or move quickly away from the source of the smell and trouble. Take the paintbrush to an undisturbed colony of aphids and see how close it needs to be before they smell the pheromone and react.

Honeydew poo

Look closely at your herd and you might see droplets of shiny liquid oozing out of the aphids' bottoms. This is aphid poo and it's called honeydew. Aphids feed by tapping into a plant's plumbing system to steal a sugary liquid called sap, which is made in leaves and carried around the plant in veins. The sap is full of sugar but has little protein, so aphids must swallow a great deal of it to get all the nutrients they need. The excess sugar and water pass out of the other end as sticky honeydew.

Husks

Some of your aphids may stop moving and change colour. Look closer – you may find that the body is just an empty husk with a tiny hole in its abdomen. This "mummy" is all that's left after a parasitic grub laid by a wasp has eaten the aphid's insides, before turning into an adult wasp and escaping through the hole. It can't be a nice way to die!

Ant farmers

Some species of ants "farm" aphids to collect honeydew. The ants protect the aphids from predators and even move them around on the plant if food is drying up. In return, the aphids let the ants "milk" them like herds of cattle.

Aphid poo (honeydew)! It's a delicious and highly prized honey in many parts of the world.

21

CATERPILLARS

Caterpillars turn into butterflies or moths, this we know; but how do they actually get there? The magical transformation is one of nature's great miracles, and it's also something that anybody – given a few bits of basic information – can witness first-hand by rearing caterpillars at home. All you have to do is find a few caterpillars (most species will do) and keep them well fed. But be warned: caterpillars are hungry animals!

CREATURE FEATURES

SETAE

Caterpillars have lots of sensory hairs called setae that detect objects and vibrations.

ABDOMEN

Life cycle

The life cycle of butterflies involves what we call "complete metamorphosis", which means the adult and juvenile stages are totally different. Insects that undergo complete metamorphosis actually have four stages in their life cycle: **egg, larva, pupa,** and **adult.**

LIFE CYCLE

Egg

Larva
(caterpillar)

Pupa
(chrysalis)

Adult
(butterfly)

Red admiral
butterfly

Hatching out

Caterpillars are really just food-processing units, their job being simply to eat and grow. After hatching out, tiny new caterpillars are only a few millimetres long and usually have to eat their own egg (some species die if they don't). Once they've nibbled their way out, the feasting begins in earnest...

Between hatching and their final moult, caterpillars balloon in weight. Hawkmoth caterpillars multiply in weight 10,000 times in only 20 days! Though their bodies are soft, caterpillars do have exoskeletons (albeit stretchy ones) that limit growth. As a result, they must moult 4–5 times as they grow. The final moult reveals a chrysalis or pupa, and it is inside this that the last and most miraculous change takes place.

Owl butterfly caterpillar

TUBERCLE
Many caterpillars have wart-like bumps called tubercles. The tubercles often have spines or hairs which are sometimes (but not always) poisonous or able to sting.

Tussah silk moth caterpillar

THORAX

ANTENNA

HEAD

TRUE LEGS
Count the legs. You might find as many as 16, but caterpillars are insects and insects should only have six! So what's going on? Well, at the front of the body are the six "true legs", which look like normal insect legs and have joints.

FALSE LEGS
The five pairs of legs behind the true legs are called false legs or prolegs. These remind me of jelly-baby limbs, all short and squishy. Each ends in a fringe of tiny velcro-like hooks called crochets.

SPIRACLES
Look carefully along the side of a caterpillar and you'll see breathing holes, or spiracles, on each segment. These let air into breathing tubes that run throughout the body.

EYES
There are clusters of very simple eyes called ocelli on either side of the head. They can't "see" well but can tell the difference between light and dark.

MANDIBLE (JAW)

Fifth instar

First instar

Monarch caterpillar

onarch caterpillars take only two weeks o reach full size, moulting four times on he way. The different stages between oults are known as "instars".

MOUTHPARTS
Caterpillars have jaws called mandibles that work side to side to slice up leaves. Under these are the maxillae, a pair of smaller jaws that taste food and make sure it's up to standard.

23

THE "PILLA VILLA"

In the wild, caterpillars live in a salad bowl and need never move far for their next mouthful, which is something to bear in mind when you rear them in captivity. As well as providing plenty of fresh food, you'll need to prevent your pilla villa from becoming stale or too humid, which can encourage bacteria and fungi – two of the caterpillar farmer's biggest enemies.

The easy way to get caterpillars is to buy them by mail order! There are lots of butterfly suppliers who will post eggs, caterpillars, or pupae to you. It's cheating but it's a good way to obtain exotic species that you'd never find at home.

Finding caterpillars

You can find caterpillars by searching the undersides of leaves on plants and bushes in spring and summer. Another technique is to do a little "bush beating". Place a white sheet or upturned umbrella under a branch and give the plant a good thwack with a stick. Any insects, including caterpillars, will drop off. But the best way to collect caterpillars is to watch out for female butterflies laying eggs and then collect these. This way, you'll know exactly what species you've got.

Use a paintbrush to nudge your caterpillars if you need to move them.

BUILDING AN ENCLOSURE

As they grow, caterpillars will need larger containers. For eggs and tiny caterpillars I use small plastic boxes lined with kitchen towel. These can get sweaty due to condensation, so to improve ventilation, cut a hole out of the lid, stretch netting across, and clip the lid back on. Larger caterpillars need taller containers that can house plants in a vase or jar of water. A varnished cardboard box (right) works well. Alternatively, make a cylindrical insect house from a biscuit tin (see page 48).

1. *To make* a caterpillar house from a cardboard box, start by cutting a window in one side. If you're using a shoe box, cut a window in the lid. The window will go at the front.

2. *Waterproof* the inside and outside of the box with a coat of quick-drying varnish. This stops it getting damp and falling apart.

A plastic tub makes a good home for smallish caterpillars.

3. *Line the window* with fine netting from a fabric shop or an old stocking. Black netting is best as it's easy to see through. If you don't have a shoe box, make a cardboard frame to hold the netting in place.

4. *Line the floor* with tissue and put in a suitable plant. The leaves must touch the sides of the box so wandering caterpillars can always find them. Plug the vase or jar with wool or Plasticine to stop the caterpillars drowning.

Feeding

Your caterpillars will need a regular supply of the right kind of plant. To replace the chewed old plant material, put fresh new stems in with it and then wait an hour or so for the caterpillars to walk onto the new stuff. Then carefully remove the old plant. Any stray caterpillars can be gently lifted across, but if they're about to moult (see right), don't touch them! Instead, keep the bit of stem they're on.

CATERPILLAR HOUSE

Fresh food

Tussah silk moth caterpillar

Mucking out

Caterpillars, being eating machines, make a lot of droppings (the technical word for which is frass). Your caterpillar house will need mucking out every day at least to keep things clean and prevent disease. Throw away the paper towel and frass, wipe down the inside of the box, and then re-line with new paper towel. Easy!

Frass

I'll have the next size up please!

If a caterpillar isn't moving or looks off-colour, it may be about to moult. There may be a bulge behind the head, and if you touch the caterpillar it may simply move from side to side rather than flee. Moving your caterpillar at this point may damage or even kill it, so leave it in place and keep an eye on it. When they're about to moult, most caterpillars spin a little silk pad that's difficult to see (unless it's on the side of the container). The caterpillar then hooks its rear feet to this silk. A Y-shaped split opens up on the head capsule, and the "new" caterpillar, in a fresh and bigger skin, crawls out, leaving the old skin attached to the silk pad. After a little rest, while it waits for its new, soft skin to harden up, the caterpillar returns to doing what it does best: stuffing its face.

Emperor moth caterpillar (5th instar)

Moulted skin

A caterpillar has around 4000 muscles in its body, of which more than 200 are in its head. A human has at most 850!

CHRYSALISES

When your caterpillars have got so big they can't stuff another leaf past their mandibles, something odd happens. Butterfly caterpillars go off their food, stop moving, and may hang from a leaf or lasso themselves to a stem. Moth caterpillars may start racing around their cage, trying to find some soil in which to bury themselves, or may enclose themselves in a cocoon of silk or leaves.

Small tortoiseshell caterpillar

The caterpillars are getting ready for the next change and will soon shed the last of their skins to reveal something totally different: a **chrysalis** (in butterflies) or a **pupa** (in moths). Keep checking your caterpillar when it's ready to start this process as it's well worth watching. If you haven't identified the species, give it plenty of options: put some twigs, some bark, and a good 5–8 cm (2–3 in) of soil in its cage.

Swallowtail butterfly

MAKE A CHRYSALIS TREE

Life goes on beneath the chrysalis skin, but other than an occasional wiggle or squeak, there's little activity. This stage can last a few weeks or, if the chrysalises form in autumn, probably a whole winter. Butterfly chrysalises should remain on their twigs, but you can snip off the twigs and pin them to a board or a more robust branch if you want. Make sure the emerging butterflies will have room to perch and stretch their wings. If necessary, you can remove chrysalises from their silk pads and reattach them to a new support with wool (below).

1.

*A **chrysalis** that has attached itself to a container is best left in place, but if you have move it, tease it gently away from the silk pad.*

Swallowtail caterpillars attach their rear end to a pad of silk on a stem and then spin what looks like a seatbelt to hold themselves in place.

The skin splits behind the head, and what bulges out is not very caterpillar-like at all! The chrysalis is soft and flexible and wriggles to push the old skin backwards.

2.

*Pull the **cremaster** (tail) through some cotton wool so that the tiny hooks catch threads of cotton.*

The skin wrinkles like a sock. When it gets to the end, the chrysalis unhooks its tail, flicks aside the skin, and reattaches to the silk pad with a velcro-like tip called a cremaster.

The real magic now begins. Inside the chrysalis, the cells of the caterpillar break down into a kind of living soup and then reorganize themselves into a completely new body form: a butterfly.

3.

*Glue the **wool** to a twig using a tiny dab of superglue so that the chrysalis hangs naturally. Make sure there is room for the emerging butterfly.*

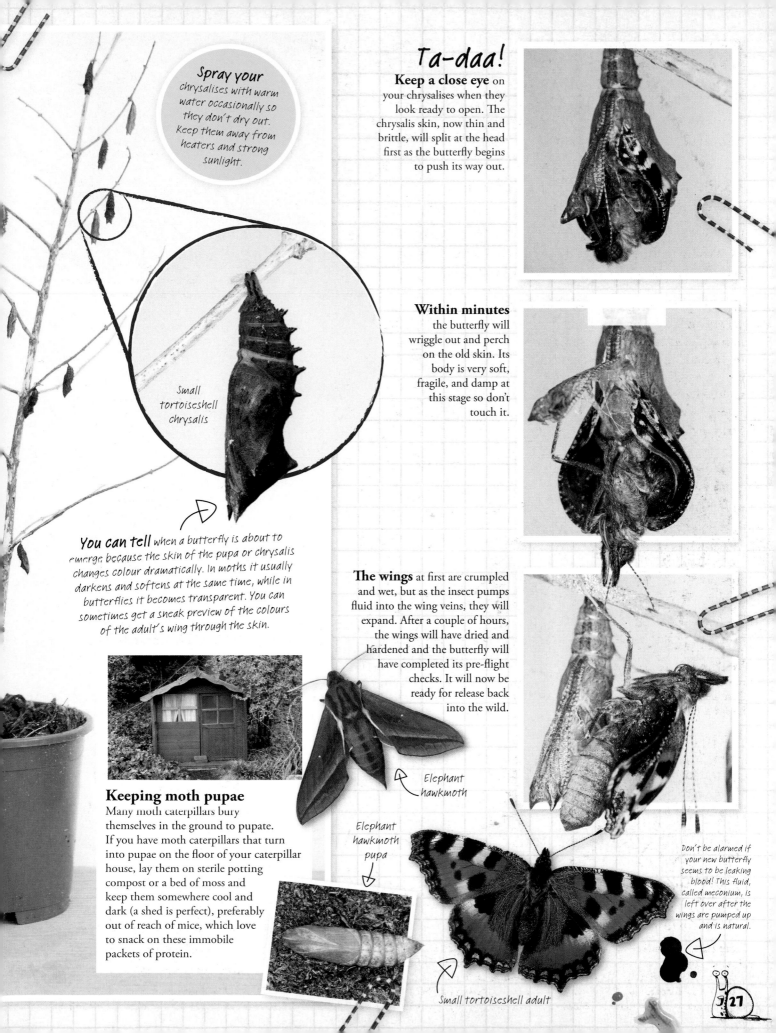

Spray your chrysalises with warm water occasionally so they don't dry out. Keep them away from heaters and strong sunlight.

Ta-daa!

Keep a close eye on your chrysalises when they look ready to open. The chrysalis skin, now thin and brittle, will split at the head first as the butterfly begins to push its way out.

Within minutes the butterfly will wriggle out and perch on the old skin. Its body is very soft, fragile, and damp at this stage so don't touch it.

Small tortoiseshell chrysalis

You can tell when a butterfly is about to emerge because the skin of the pupa or chrysalis changes colour dramatically. In moths it usually darkens and softens at the same time, while in butterflies it becomes transparent. You can sometimes get a sneak preview of the colours of the adult's wing through the skin.

The wings at first are crumpled and wet, but as the insect pumps fluid into the wing veins, they will expand. After a couple of hours, the wings will have dried and hardened and the butterfly will have completed its pre-flight checks. It will now be ready for release back into the wild.

Keeping moth pupae

Many moth caterpillars bury themselves in the ground to pupate. If you have moth caterpillars that turn into pupae on the floor of your caterpillar house, lay them on sterile potting compost or a bed of moss and keep them somewhere cool and dark (a shed is perfect), preferably out of reach of mice, which love to snack on these immobile packets of protein.

Elephant hawkmoth

Elephant hawkmoth pupa

Don't be alarmed if your new butterfly seems to be leaking blood! This fluid, called meconium, is left over after the wings are pumped up and is natural.

Small tortoiseshell adult

27

WORMS

The earthworm is one of the simplest animals you can keep in a bug zoo. It has no eyes, no ears, no legs, no face, and no limbs of any kind. Yet this lowly creature has more ecological importance than anything else in this book, and for that reason alone it's worth including in your collection. Worms are very easy to keep. The biggest problem is actually seeing what they're up to because worms, being worms, will do what they're good at – and that's burrowing! But even if you don't get to see much of your exhibits, you can still find out why these natural recyclers are so good at improving soil.

Record breakers
There are giant earthworm species that can grow to 4 metres (13 ft) in length, such as the Gripsland earthworm of Australia and the Mekong giant earthworm of Asia.

SKIN
The skin of a worm is its eyes, ears, nose, and tongue all in one. Every square millimetre has more than 700 taste receptors, making worms very sensitive to what's going on around them. Worms can't see, but they do have many light-sensitive cells on the surface of their skin.

CREATURE FEATURES

ANUS

TAIL END
The tail end is usually flatter and almost paddle shaped and can be expanded to wedge a worm into its hole. Many species reach out of their burrows on warm, wet nights, keeping their tail in the burrow like an anchor, and at the slightest disturbance they can withdraw by tightening up their muscles.

SETAE
Each segment has four pairs of small, stiff bristles called "setae", used to grip the walls of burrows (handy when a bird is tugging the other end). You can feel them if you pull a worm gently through your fingers. Put a worm on dry paper and the setae make a scratchy sound.

Is the worm above male or female?

HEAD END

All the vital organs are in the front section between the mouth and the saddle. In here are the worm's five hearts, its brain, its stomach, and the reproductive bits. While it's not true that cutting a worm in half will give you two worms, the front section can survive and grow a new tail.

SADDLE

The saddle is the most obvious feature on an adult worm. This thickened organ produces a slimy glue that holds worms together when they mate. When a worm lays eggs, the saddle slides off to form a capsule around them.

SEGMENTS

MOUTH

Brandling worm
(*Eisenia fetida*)

One of the easiest species to find is the brandling worm, also known as the tiger worm because of its distinctive stripy appearance. When threatened, it produces a yellow fluid that smells bad, which is possibly why it's also known as the garlic worm. Brandling worms are found in heaps of rotting plant material, especially compost heaps.

Night crawler
(*Lumbricus terrestris*)

This is one of the biggest of the garden worm species and can reach 30 cm (1 ft) long. Night crawlers hide in deep burrows during the day, but you can find them on lawns on warm, wet nights when they come up to find fresh food. Tread carefully if you look for them – they are incredibly shy and quickly dart back underground.

Black head
(*Aporrectodea longa*)

This is the species responsible for making worm casts on your lawn. These squiggly heaps of what looks like fine soil are little piles of worm poo! Black heads are handsome worms with a dark grey head end, and they make good guests in a wormery. You might even get to watch them make their casts.

Worm hunting

You can find worms under rocks and flowerpots at any time, but the best time to hunt them is on damp summer nights, when the really big worms come out of the ground to search for fresh food. Earthworms can't see the colour red, so a torch covered with a red filter makes a handy hunting tool. To find brandling worms, rummage through a compost bin.

MAKING A WORMERY

A wormery can be as simple as a large jar (giant pickle jars work well) or a plastic tub. What you put in your wormery depends on what type of worm you've got: brandling worms prefer rotting plant material, other types of worms need some soil.

The deluxe wormery

The only problem with using a jar as a wormery is that your worms can hide in the middle where you won't see them. The deluxe wormery allows you to view your captives much more frequently. You don't need to be good at carpentry to make the one shown here as it's very simple. All it requires is a strip of wood (the thinner the better), a sheet of perspex, and four big bulldog clips.

1. **Ask** an adult to cut the perspex into squares about 30 cm (12 in) wide and to cut the wood into three batons to form a frame that fits the perspex squares.

2. **Place** the other perspex square on top to sandwich the wooden frame between the two clear sheets.

3. **Clip** the corners to hold everything together. Ta da! You have now built a wormery. If the bulldog clips are large enough, the wormery should stand up on its own.

Feeding
Leaf litter, potato peel, and grass clippings all make good worm food. Leave them on the surface and the worms will do the rest. Bear in mind a worm can eat more than half its body weight in food in a day – so they'll need lots of food!

If your worms try t escape, block the te with Plasticine.

Add Worms

WORM ENCLOSURE

4. **Fill** with different layers of soil, potting compost, and sand. These layers will get stirred around by your worms, revealing just how good they are at moving the soil. Finish off with a layer of leaf litter or grass cuttings on top, then water your wormery to make the soil damp. Then add your worms!

5. Make a black curtain from card or cover the wormery with lightproof cloth. This keeps the soil dark and will mean the worms are not shy of wriggling next to the perspex, where you can see them.

Digging machines

An acre of pasture contains up to 3 million worms that dig about 15 km (9 miles) of tunnels a day! You can watch these digging machines in action inside your wormery. They move by using muscles to squeeze fluid into different parts of the body. First fluid is pumped into the streamlined head end to make it stretch out into the soil. Then more fluid is pumped in to make the head expand and force the soil apart.

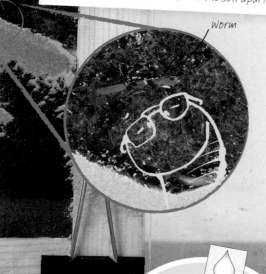

Worm

Moisture

A worm's body is 75–90 per cent water, and for this reason it's important you don't let your wormery dry out. Keep the soil damp but not soggy. Waterlogged soil contains very little oxygen and will cause the worms to suffocate or drown.

Poo factory

Worms do a great job of improving soil. As well as stirring it up with all their digging, they recycle dead matter by eating it and turning it into worm poo – the perfect compost for plants! You can manufacture worm compost by making a wormery from plastic boxes. This kind of wormery works best with brandling worms (*Eisenia fetida*). They love all sorts of dead plant material from rotten fruit and potato peelings to soggy leaves.

1. Ask an adult to cut a hole in the bottom of a plastic box, leaving a wide frame around the hole.

2. Place a grill in the bottom of the box over the hole. Worm poo will fall through this grill.

3. Stack your box in an empty one with space below to collect compost.

4. Fill the top box with peelings or leaves (not soil), and add your worms. Make ventilation holes or a netting window in the lid and put the lid on.

Worm poo

Old carrot peelings

LOOK OUT FOR

Eggs and babies

If you pick through your poo factory carefully, you might notice worm eggs. These are tiny little almost lemon-shaped cocoons. If you hold them up to the light and examine them with a magnifying lens, you might be able to see the brand new brandlings inside. When your wormery is established, you'll also find dozens of baby worms squirming in the gunk.

Baby worm

See-through worm

Put a worm on a torch and examine it with a hand lens for a look inside the worm's body! You'll see the worm's squiggly gut as a dark silhouette, with a bright red blood vessel running along it. Watch the blood vessel pulse as blood squidges along it. You might be able to see the five hearts causing this blood rush – they will show up as thickened red splodges towards the head. Lots of small white tubes called nephridia (which work like kidneys) may be visible, as well as two pairs of white calcium sacks, which are thought to be involved with digestion and maybe reproduction.

31

EARWIGS

These shy creatures are common enough and are usually seen scuttling for cover when disturbed. They are instantly recognizable thanks to that most distinctive of features: the "pincers" that protrude from their rear ends. But what else do you know about earwigs? Earwigs have a PR problem because people think they crawl inside your ear and eat your brain – not true. They're not even that much of a pest in the garden. Get to know them and you'll find they make great little additions to your bug zoo.

CREATURE FEATURES

ANTENNA

EYE

MOUTH

PALP

HEAD

THORAX

Earwigs are flattened in profile, allowing them to squeeze easily under and between things. They love hiding in tight crevices and can often be found lurking under rocks.

Why are they called "earwigs"?

Some say it's because the flying wings look ear shaped when unfolded, giving you "earwing" – a nice idea, but unlikely, since these are rarely seen. Others suggest it's because the pincers look a little like ear-piercing tools. Many of the names given to them in other countries back this up, for example, *perce-oreille* (ear piercer) in French. They were called *earwicga* in old English, and *ohrwurm* in German – which mean "ear creature" and "ear worm" respectively. These names are probably a reference to them crawling into tight, dark places, such as inside ears, which probably happened quite often when we used to sleep on mattresses stuffed with hay.

Grrr...

Bamboo canes can be used to make an earwiggery – see over the page. Earwigs often hide in these in the garden.

WINGS

The wings are hidden under wing covers, or elytra. Earwigs can fly, but their wings are folded so intricately (40 times) that it takes ages to unpack them.

There are 1900 species of earwig in the world, but the common earwig (Forficula auricularia) is the one you see most often. Originally from Europe, it is now found on every continent except Antarctica.

LEGS (6)

PINCERS

Earwigs use their pincers, or "cerci", for a multitude of tasks, including defence (they threaten and try to nip but cannot generate enough force to hurt), unfolding the very complex wings, subduing struggling prey, and (probably) breeding.

Mr and Mrs Earwig can be told apart by the size and shape of their pincers. Males have large, very curved ones, while the females have narrower and straighter ones.

ABDOMEN

The male has ten visible segments while females have only eight.

Male

Female

MAKING AN EARWIGGERY

Earwigs are "thigmotaxic", which means they can't stand open spaces and don't relax unless their bodies are pressed tightly against a surface. They are also nocturnal. So the challenge to a bug zoo keeper is to keep these animals happy and behaving naturally in captivity while also being able to see what they're getting up to. For that reason, a little bit of thought and effort needs to be given to the construction of your "earwiggery".

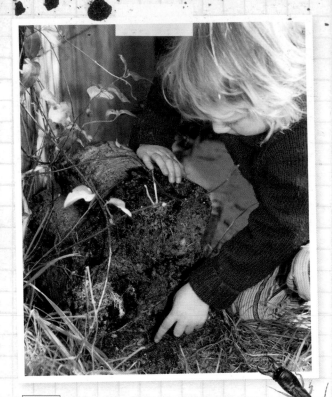

Catching an earwig

Earwigs are not hard to find but they move fast when discovered! They like to hide in dry, dark places but some locations are earwiggier than others. Look under logs (particularly any with loose bark) piles of bricks, plant pots, and even inside dead hollow plant stems. In the winter you can often find hibernating earwigs by splitting the stems lengthways. There may be other insects hiding there too.

You can trap earwigs with a flowerpot. Block the hole in the bottom and fill with straw. Dribble a little honey onto the straw and upend the whole thing onto a short garden cane. Place it near the compost heap or among the flower beds. After a week, several earwigs will have taken up residence in your trap.

Alternatively, stack sheets of cardboard on a garden cane and use this to stake them to the ground so they don't blow away. Many insects, including earwigs, will move into this high-rise bug hotel.

EARWIG ENCLOSURE

1. Collect some hollow stems or canes. Get an adult to split them in half for you. Scrape out any pith, then glue them to the lid or sides of a clear box using water-based or PVA glue.

Use an old chocolate box

2. Spread a little damp soil, moss, or leaf litter over the base of your container. This will keep the atmosphere humid, but don't add too much or the earwigs will burrow into it and you won't be able to watch them.

3. Add your earwigs, then replace the lid. Cover the lid with card to make it dark. The earwigs will squeeze into the pieces of split cane, allowing you to peel back the curtain and find them!

Snug as a bug in a rug!

Little is known about earwigs, so anything you witness in your earwig enclosure is worth recording. I've never seen them mate, but apparently the females choose the males with the biggest pincers. After mating, the female excavates a burrow for her eggs. She lays 30–50 eggs and tends them vigilantly, often licking them or moving them around the burrow. When they hatch she continues to brood them, bringing the babies food until they're old enough to leave the nest.

Feeding

Earwigs have a wide range of tastes and will eat many things, both living and dead. Their favourite place for dining out is a compost heap. Here they can find other small creatures and their eggs and larvae, as well as loads of rotting plant material, algae, and fungi. Try experimenting with your earwigs' menu to see what they prefer.

Cucumber

Water is very

important to earwigs, so it helps to keep the atmosphere humid – not so wet that everything goes mouldy, but not bone dry either. Pop in a small dish of water-soaked cotton wool, moss, or kitchen towel to make sure they don't get thirsty.

LADYBIRDS

I find it hard to resist correcting people when I hear them talking about ladybirds as cute little beetles. Sure they're good for the garden, and yes the majority of them (not all) have bright and perky colours. But these predators are not as ladylike or as gentle as we've been led to think. Watching a ladybird mow its way through a herd of greenfly is like watching a horror film, with bits of greenfly flying everywhere, and plenty of blood and gore too. You have been warned. Keeping ladybirds is not for the squeamish.

Common ladybirds

7-spot ladybird
(*Coccinella septempunctata*)
This is the iconic ladybird and the one that gives the family its common name, the seven spots symbolizing Our Lady's seven sorrows. It is native to Europe but found across the globe.

22-spot ladybird
(*Psyllobora vigintiduo-punctata*)
One of several species that do not have red as a background colour, the 22-spot is also unusual in that it is not a predator and feeds on mildew (mould). It is native to Europe.

Harlequin ladybird
(*Harmonia axyridis*)
This large species gets its name because it comes in a huge variety of colours and patterns. Originally from Asia, it has spread around the world and earned itself a bad reputation for preying on native ladybird species.

CREATURE FEATURES

HEAD
ELYTRON
WING
LEG
ABDOMEN

HEAD
EYES
MOUTHPARTS
PRONOTUM

Don't mistake the large white marks at the front for eyes! They are simply coloured marks on the pronotum – the front part of the thorax. The actual head of the ladybird is much smaller.

CATCHING YOUR BEAST

In summer you can find ladybirds by searching with your eyes through garden plants such as roses, beans, sweet peas, or even stinging nettles (wear gloves so you don't get stung). Because these beetles are so brightly coloured, they stand out and are easy to see. The larvae and pupae can be found the same way.

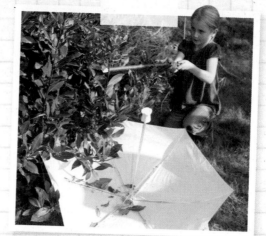

To find less common species, place a white sheet or umbrella under a bush and shake the leaves. Insects will fall onto the sheet. Transport your ladybirds home in a jar, but keep any larvae you find in separate containers as they have a tendency to be cannibalistic.

Keep me well stocked with aphids, I eat a lot!

LADYBIRD ENCLOSURE

Most ladybirds can be easily kept in simple containers. Any small, transparent container will do. A 10 cm (4 in) wide dish can house up to 15 ladybirds, but I tend to keep 5 per dish – otherwise you'll have to find a lot of food!

1.

Line an empty container with kitchen towel and stock it with aphids and some vegetation for the ladybirds to climb on.

2.

Transfer the ladybirds to their new home. Use a paintbrush to move them without injuring them. Don't forget to put the lid on afterwards!

This ladybird is eating an aphid. Turn the page to see this in more detail!

Dead aphids

Cleaning

Ladybirds are very vulnerable to disease caused by bacteria or fungi, so a daily clean-up to remove dead aphids and other debris is recommended. Ideally, cycle your ladybirds between two containers, cleaning out the used one each time you empty it.

Keep an eye open for eggs. Ladybirds tend to lay their clutches of skittle-shaped eggs on the sides of the container. When the young hatch they like to make a first meal of their eggshells. Don't give them aphids until they've walked away from the eggshells.

FEEDING TIME

Ladybirds are predators. The larvae and the adults both prey on aphids – the tiny sap-sucking insects, also called greenflies or blackflies, that infest garden plants. The biggest challenge you'll have as a ladybird farmer is keeping your beetles in food, and that means you either have to be a dedicated aphid hunter and gatherer or an aphid farmer too. These weird little unloved but incredibly successful insects are fascinating in their own right, so I've dedicated a section entirely to them (see page 18).

Good places to find aphids are the fresh growing tips or buds of roses, beans, and sweet peas; the undersides of sycamore (maple) and lime tree leaves; thistles; and probably the most reliable – stinging nettles (wear gloves if you handle these). There are two ways of harvesting the aphids. One is to use scissors to snip off a whole stem. The other is to use a paintbrush to knock aphids off one by one.

Cut a piece of stem that's infested with aphids. Make sure it's small enough to fit inside your ladybird enclosure.

Sweet pea plant

To harvest aphids with a paintbrush, hold a pot or jar underneath the colony and gently sweep them off.

A pair of ladybirds will need at least 20 aphids a day to keep them in tip-top breeding condition.

Look out for an oily liquid coming out of the pointy "cornicles" on the rear end of aphids when they're under attack. This is a defensive chemical used to ward off ladybirds.

I'm off.

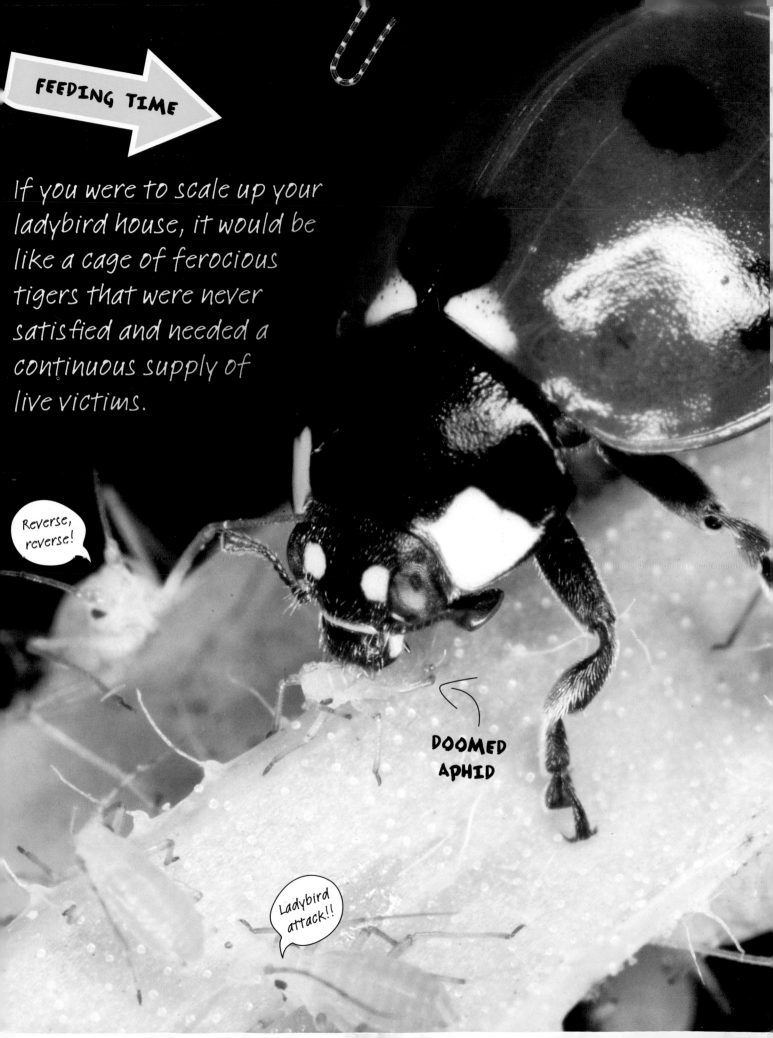

FROM EGG TO EATING MACHINE

If your ladybirds are happy, well fed and not all ladies (or men), you will possibly get eggs. Some species will lay eggs only during spring or early summer, while others, such as the 7-spot ladybird, breed continuously if they have enough light, warmth, and food. Look after your "baby birds" well and you can **watch the whole life cycle unfold** before your eyes.

Close-up of a ladybird larva

2. Once they've eaten their own eggshells, they start their marauding lifestyle. At first they're dwarfed by full-grown aphids, but they will climb on top and, while riding piggyback, bite into the aphid and suck its blood – vampire jockeys!

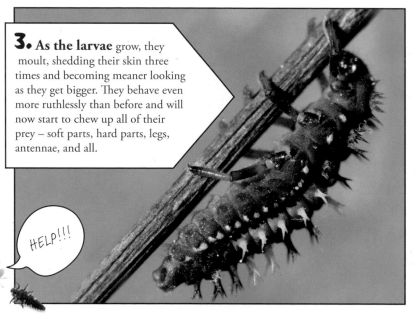

3. As the larvae grow, they moult, shedding their skin three times and becoming meaner looking as they get bigger. They behave even more ruthlessly than before and will now start to chew up all of their prey – soft parts, hard parts, legs, antennae, and all.

HELP!!!

5. The pupa remains in place while the beetle within takes shape. Then, after a couple of weeks, out pops a ladybird. But it looks unlike any ladybird you've ever seen – has there been a terrible mix-up in the body shop? It's not red and black but a pale, washed-out yellow. And where's that smooth, domed back formed from the glossy wing cases? Instead, this little, damp, crumpled creature staggers out and sits there...

6. Over the next few hours, the saggy, baggy wings and wing cases slowly pump up, and the ladybird starts to take shape.

1. **The eggs** are laid in clutches of up to 300. (It's best to separate eggs and adults at this stage so the adults don't eat them.) A week later, they hatch and you get your first look at a "baby bird". These odd little things look like evil caterpillars, and I guess that's what they are.

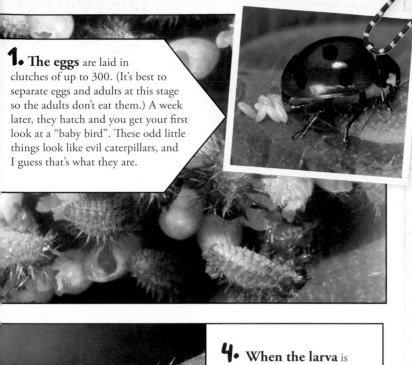

Chemical weapons

The bright colours of ladybirds make them stand out to our eyes. In nature, animals often use bright colours like these to advertise how poisonous or foul tasting they are. Ladybirds are no exception – **apparently they taste horrid and bitter.**

And that's not the only defensive trick they have up their sleeves...

If harassed by ants, ladybirds clamp their bodies down, hiding their legs under their impenetrable wing cases. The legs tuck neatly into grooves on the underside of the thorax and abdomen, leaving no fragile bits sticking out.

4. **When the larva** is about 2 weeks old, its skin splits for the last time and, just as with caterpillars, a pupa emerges. Attached by the tip of its abdomen to a plant or the container, it sits still unless bothered by a curious poke with a paintbrush, when it will twitch its head end up and down. It is thought this is a defence against parasites and predators.

If the clamp-down fails, ladybirds leak. Yep, they ooze a foul-tasting and foul-smelling liquid – a defensive technique known as "reflex bleeding". If you pick up a ladybird, you'll see the stuff staining your fingers. The liquid oozes out of leg joints and passes along grooves in the body, quickly coating the ladybird in a bitter mixture containing protective chemicals called alkaloids. Despite this, some animals will quite happily eat them. Maybe they like their food a little tangy?

Don't prod me too hard!

7. **Next,** the wing cases and pronotum blush and colour up (which might take a few days to do completely). When they have dried and hardened, it's off again on the hunt for more aphids to victimize.

Ooze

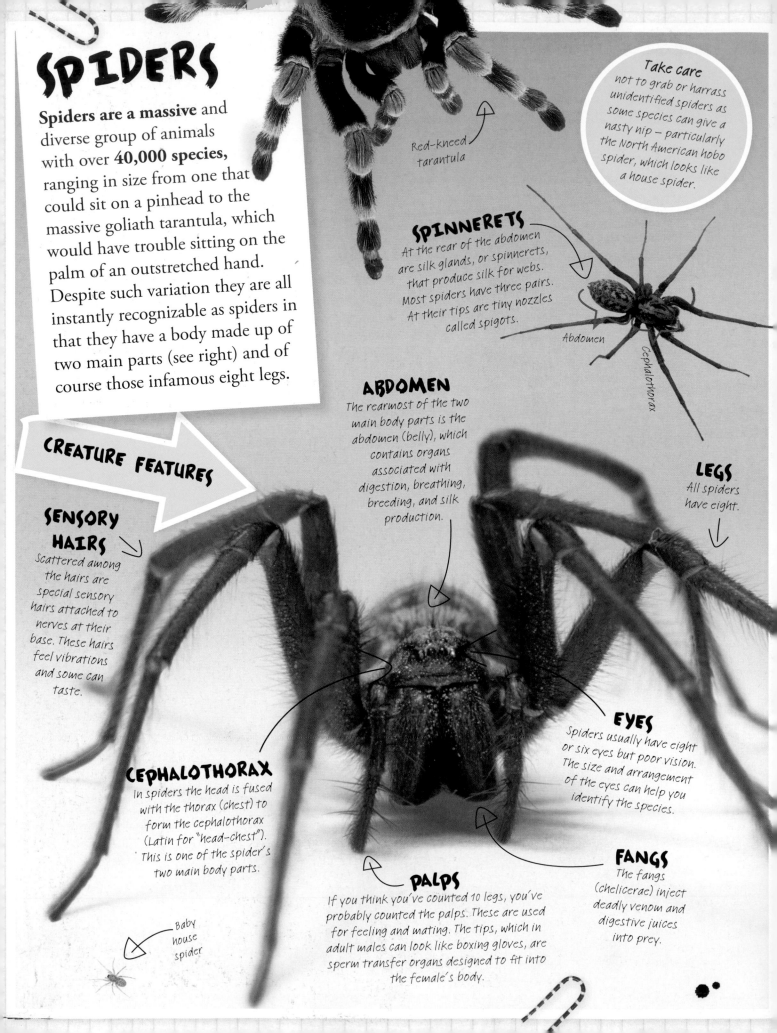

SPIDERS

Spiders are a massive and diverse group of animals with over **40,000 species**, ranging in size from one that could sit on a pinhead to the massive goliath tarantula, which would have trouble sitting on the palm of an outstretched hand. Despite such variation they are all instantly recognizable as spiders in that they have a body made up of two main parts (see right) and of course those infamous eight legs.

Red-kneed tarantula

Take care not to grab or harrass unidentified spiders as some species can give a nasty nip – particularly the North American hobo spider, which looks like a house spider.

SPINNERETS
At the rear of the abdomen are silk glands, or spinnerets, that produce silk for webs. Most spiders have three pairs. At their tips are tiny nozzles called spigots.

Abdomen

Cephalothorax

ABDOMEN
The rearmost of the two main body parts is the abdomen (belly), which contains organs associated with digestion, breathing, breeding, and silk production.

CREATURE FEATURES

LEGS
All spiders have eight.

SENSORY HAIRS
Scattered among the hairs are special sensory hairs attached to nerves at their base. These hairs feel vibrations and some can taste.

EYES
Spiders usually have eight or six eyes but poor vision. The size and arrangement of the eyes can help you identify the species.

CEPHALOTHORAX
In spiders the head is fused with the thorax (chest) to form the cephalothorax (Latin for "head-chest"). This is one of the spider's two main body parts.

FANGS
The fangs (chelicerae) inject deadly venom and digestive juices into prey.

Baby house spider

PALPS
If you think you've counted 10 legs, you've probably counted the palps. These are used for feeling and mating. The tips, which in adult males can look like boxing gloves, are sperm transfer organs designed to fit into the female's body.

WHO TO KEEP

Tegenaria domestica

Pardosa monticola

Pholcus

House spider ✓

The European house spider (*Tegenaria domestica*), which is common across Europe and North America, is easy to keep and makes a great pet. Even better is its larger cousin the giant house spider (*Tegenaria duellica*). These are the most entertaining as you get to see all the lovely details of your animal and its behaviour.

Wolf spiders ✓

The free-ranging wolf spiders make the best spider pets. To keep these you need to add a little soil or compost to your spider house, and you could try planting some living plants and adding other "furniture" to make it really interesting for both you and your captive.

Daddy-long-legs ✓

Another spider you're likely to find at home is the daddy-long-legs spider (*Pholcus*), which makes fine, tangled cobwebs high in the corners of our rooms. It makes an interesting pet and is easier to find than *Tegenaria*.

Garden spider ✗

The garden spider is common across the world and catches prey in that classic doily of death, the orb web. But garden spiders need a lot of room to make their webs, so they are not well suited to life in an animal tank.

HOW TO CATCH 'EM

Tegenaria

 Even the most tidy house has quiet corners where spiders lurk. Try behind the TV, the sofa, in the broom cupboard, under the stairs, or in the garden shed. Look for webs and use a pocket torch – *Tegenaria* likes to hide in dark recesses.

Tegenaria is tricky to catch. Its sensory hairs make it incredibly sensitive to vibration – just a careless sigh from the spider hunter could send it scuttling into an inconvenient recess. Try and predict its direction of travel and have ready a container with a close-fitting lid.

Use a paintbrush or a pencil to gently poke Tegeneria out of its web or recess. Don't worry about damaging the web – it will make another one for you anyway.

Daddy-long-legs spiders are easy to catch. Rather than running away they do a strange little dance, shaking their bodies about so quickly that they become a blur. This makes them difficult to pick up if you're a bird with nothing but a beak, but it's dead easy if you have a jam jar!

THE HOUSE SPIDER HOUSE

Setting up a house for a house spider (*Tegenaria*) couldn't be simpler. I use a plastic animal tank with a close-fitting lid. If you like, add "furniture" to act as a lair – a piece of bark or broken flower pot is perfect. Keep the tank away from direct sunlight and add a wad of damp moss. Keep this moist at all times so the spider can drink when it needs to. I also spray with a mist sprayer once a day.

1. Release your captive into its new home and quickly close the lid. Your spider will soon make itself at home, or rather make itself **a** home – within an hour or so you might notice a very light and fine framework of a web.

Old food

2. Over the next few weeks your spider will build up its web until it's created quite a work of art. It might look like a random tangle, but watch how your spider uses it – you'll realize it has order and function. You might have to view your spider at night to see it out and about. Try and identify which bits of web it waits on, where its lair is, and what it does with its food. It's handy from time to time to remove old prey items or moulted skins. This can by fiddly, so I like to use long tweezers or chopsticks to pick out the bits.

Finding food

Anything a spider can overpower is prey. House spiders normally feed on moths or flies, and you can provide either, but flies are easiest. To harvest them, leave food or compost outside to rot, and sweep up visiting flies in a net. You can also catch flies resting on the wall by placing a jar over them. Then slip paper or card between the jar and wall to trap them.

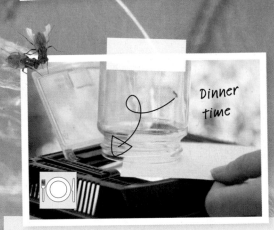

Dinner time

Release a fly into the tank or, better still, throw it into the web. When the spider feels the web move, it will leap upon its prey and deliver a lethal bite. Watch the fangs in action as the spider injects the venom that paralyses and starts to digest the body. Spiders can't eat solids, so their victims must be pre-digested. The resulting juices are sucked up through the mouth and filtered through bristles and hairs – a bit like sucking minestrone soup through your teeth and avoiding the noodles!

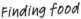
STUFF TO LOOK OUT FOR

Old skin

Moulting

If your spider goes off its food or changes colour, it may be about to moult. If you're lucky, you might see the moult take place. The spider's skin lifts off like a cap and a pale new spider bursts out, pulling all eight legs with it – like someone taking off four pairs of trousers at once!

See what happens
if you introduce lots of flies at once. Your spider may rush about collecting as many as possible, paralysing each one and then wrapping it in silk to devour later.

REENBOTTLE FLY

reeding

you keep wolf spiders, put a few together and
ey might breed. The female will carry her egg sac
ound with her (another use for silk), but after a
hile the sac will vanish and she'll look oddly hairy.
ok closer and you'll see that the "hairs" are a mass
tiny spiderlings. They cling to special, handle-like
rs on the mother's abdomen.

Drinking

Just after you've sprayed your
spider tank or refreshed the water
dish, watch out for drinking. To do
this the animal positions itself over the
water source and crouches down, pushing
the mouth onto the wet surface. Then, using
powerful sucking muscles, it slurps up the liquid.

BUSH CRICKETS

Crickets and grasshoppers often get lumped together. This isn't surprising, as they look similar and share the same powerful rear legs that make them such good leapers and so tricky to catch. But this is where the similarities really end. While grasshoppers are plant eaters, crickets are partial to snacking on other insects and even on each other. Most predatory of all, and therefore most fun to keep, are the bush crickets (known as katydids in the US).

There's no sound coming out of my mouth – it's my wings that are singing!

Great green bush cricket

ANTENNAE
Crickets have very long antennae (feelers) that may be even longer than the body.

LEGS
The back pair are modified for jumping. Just below the "knee" (middle joint) of the front leg is a sort of ear that the cricket uses to hear the songs of other crickets.

ABDOMEN

SPIRACLES
Insects breathe through small holes called spiracles. These are obvious along the abdomen of large cricket species. In some crickets you can even see the animal "breathing", the muscles in its abdomen squeezing to pump air in and out of the spiracles.

WINGS

THORAX

HEAD

OVIPOSITOR
It's easy to tell males from females as females possess a vicious-looking, sword-like appendage that sticks out from the abdomen. This is not a sting, as people often think, but a totally harmless egg-laying tube called an ovipositor.

CERCI
These little sense organs serve as feelers on the back end of the insect. They are very sensitive and are used in testing, tasting, and feeling what is going on behind the animal – a bit like reversing sensors on a car.

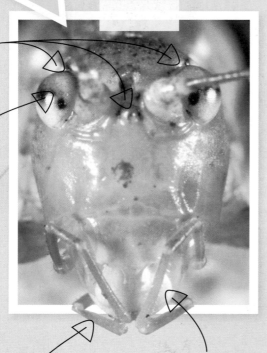

CREATURE FEATURES

OCELLI
imple eyespots, or ocelli, detect light and shade.

OMPOUND EYE
hese big, bulbous es are clusters of hundreds of tiny es (ommatidia) all working together. oth grasshoppers and crickets have excellent vision, which is partly why they're such a challenge to catch!

PALPS
These small feelers around the mouth are used to taste food.

MANDIBLES
Crickets have powerful, jagged-edged jaws that work sideways to mash and tear up food

WINGS
Most adult crickets have two pairs of wings. In some species these are used for flight, but in others they are much reduced and serve other purposes. Males use their wings to sing, or "stridulate". They do this by rubbing pegs on one wing against a reinforced vein on the other. Many crickets also hold their wings out a little while singing to form a sounding chamber.

CRICKET OR GRASSHOPPER?

Grasshoppers are herbivores and mainly eat grass. They are easily recognized by their antennae, which are shorter and thicker than crickets'. They sing differently too, by rubbing grooves on their hind legs against ribs on the wings.

True crickets, such as field crickets and house crickets, live mainly on the ground and eat both animal and plant matter. They have squat, cylindrical bodies and are never green. They are rare in the UK but can be bought from pets shops as reptile food.

Bush crickets (katydids) live in tall vegetation and are highly predatory, though they also eat plant matter. Often well camouflaged, many are bright green. Their long, whip-like antennae are longer than the body.

Collecting crickets
Crickets announce where they live by singing, but it can be very frustrating hunting them when you can hear but not see them! A good technique is to walk through long vegetation keeping your eyes on the area right in front of your feet. It's a technique called "walking them up", and it's used by cranes to hunt insects. Any insects in the grass will spring out as you get near and draw attention to themselves. All you've then got to do is grab them and put them in a jar. Another technique is to sweep a large net through long grass, and for some bush crickets, "bush beating" (see page 24) is the best answer.

CRICKET PAVILION

I find I can watch crickets for hours and hours – they are always doing something. They love to clamber around in vegetation, so you'll need to provide some form of climbing frame to create a three-dimensional habitat. Large, clear containers work best. Plastic animal tanks or cylindrical containers like the one shown here are good options. Crickets have powerful, slicing jaws, so don't rely on netting as a lid – they'll shred it and escape!

✋ Making a cricket pavilion

It's easy to make a cricket container from a biscuit or chocolates tin. You can also buy purpose-made versions, but it's cheaper to make them. You'll need a sheet of clear acetate (ask for the stiffest acetate available) from an art or craft shop or from a large stationers.

1. Ask an adult to make a few air holes in the lid of the biscuit tin. You can use either a drill or a hammer and nail to do this.

2. Roll the acetate into a cylinder so it fits tightly in the tin. Trim to size and height, but leave a 2 cm (1 in) seam. Tape or glue the seam. If you use glue, clamp the seam with clothes pegs or bulldog clips while the glue dries. Put the acetate back in the tin, pop on the lid, and you're done.

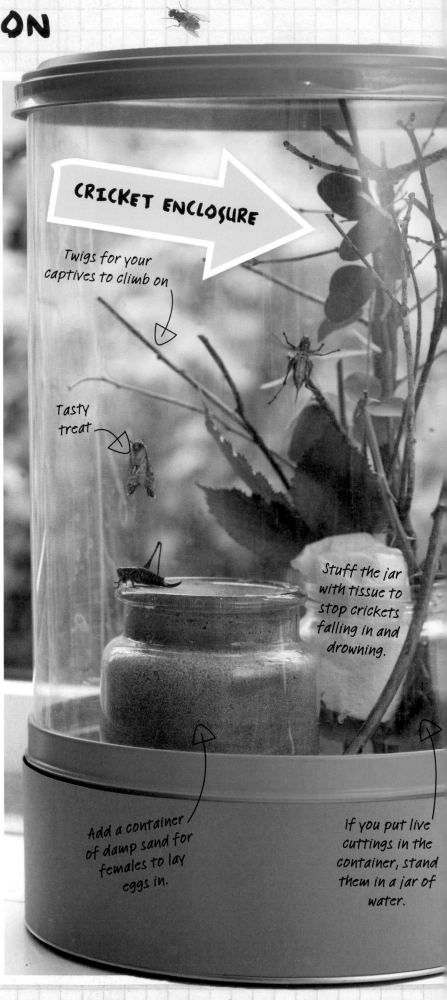

CRICKET ENCLOSURE

Twigs for your captives to climb on

Tasty treat

Stuff the jar with tissue to stop crickets falling in and drowning.

Add a container of damp sand for females to lay eggs in.

If you put live cuttings in the container, stand them in a jar of water.

🍴 **Crickets are predatory**, especially bush crickets, which makes them fun to keep, with feeding time providing a lot of action. You can give them aphids, flies, mealworms, moths, maggots, or any other small creatures. They don't just eat flesh – they like quite a varied diet and will eat a bit of everything, including some fresh greens. A selection of leaves covered with aphids makes a good three-course meal, with a main dish of insect flesh, a little side salad to nibble, and a sweet dessert of honeydew!

Blowflies

Mealworm

Decisions, decisions... What shall I have for dinner?

Water can be provided in the standard upturned bottle lid, filled with a wad of wet cotton wool or moss. A daily spray with warm water also helps.

Dark Bush cricket

LOOK OUT FOR

Growing up

Young crickets are called nymphs. When they moult for the final time and become adult, they acquire their wings, which means they can start to stridulate (sing). This is when the fun really starts and you start to see new behaviour. You may want to reorganize your set-up at this stage. Try keeping a group of females with one male and watch what happens. Does the male start singing to attract females? Does the song change when females approach him? What happens if you put two adult males in the same territory?

Moulting

This is spectacular in the big bush crickets on account of their unfeasibly long feelers! Watch the old skin split behind the head and the fresh, new insect squeeze itself out, legs, antennae, and all. Look out for bits of white, squiggly string – these are trachea, the breathing tubes of the insect that have been turned inside out. The moulting period is a sensitive time: the newly emerged cricket is soft and vulnerable (be careful not to disturb it) and runs the risk of being eaten by one of its cannibalistic housemates!

Mating

You'll almost certainly see your crickets mating, and you may even see a big white fluffy lump of gloop being produced by the male and carried by the female. This is a bag of sperm called a spermatophore and the female will use it to fertilize her eggs.

Laying

If you provide a pot of sand, you'll be able to watch females pushing their ovipositors into it to lay eggs. It's a fascinating thing to see. If you want to see the eggs, provide damp cotton wool instead of sand and look through it later with a magnifying lens.

Singing

Only male crickets sing, and they only do so when it's warm. It's said you can tell the temperature by timing a cricket's chirping. Why not use your cricket pavilion to test the theory. Count how many chirps come from a single cricket in 15 seconds. Do this a few times and work out the average. Divide this number by two and add six. In theory the answer should be the temperature in degrees Celsius! Does it work?

Gosh it's hot! Doh, ray, me, fa, so, lah....

PSEUDOSCORPIONS

These mite-munching murderers can be found anywhere and everywhere, but we seldom see them on account of their tiny size. Called pseudoscorpions, which means "false scorpions", they are every bit as spectacular as their MUCH bigger cousins. And I emphasize the word "much" because these animals are smaller than small – a big one is a mere 6 mm (0.2 in) long, and the biggest species in the world reaches only 12 mm (0.5 in).

Pseudoscorpions are members of a class of animals known as ARACHNIDS, which also includes spiders and true scorpions. Like all arachnids, pseudoscorpions have four pairs of walking legs. If you get to ogle one up close, you'll also see how they got their name: the front end looks just like a scorpion, with a pair of mean-looking pincers. It's at the other end that things look totally and obviously different – pseudoscorpions don't have a sting in their tail because they don't even have a tail! But they are **ruthless little predators** nonetheless and pack a small punch, delivering poison to their prey through the tips of the pincers. The bug zoo keeper need not worry about this as the venom is delivered in such tiny quantities that it is effective only against the pseudoscorpion's equally minuscule prey.

CREATURE FEATURES

LEGS

Being an arachnid, the pseudoscorpion has legs arranged in four pairs – that's eight in total.

To get the best out of these tiny creatures and really impress your mates, use a USB microscope to see them in their full neat and nippy glory.

ACTUAL SIZE!

PINCERS

More correctly called pedipalps, the pincers are held out when the scorpion is moving as they are covered in long sensory hairs that help the animal feel its way around. The venom gland is located in the mobile half of each claw (the "finger").

ABDOMEN

The rear part of the body is called the abdomen (or opisthoma) and is a rather dumpy, rounded, pear-shaped thing. It contains all the essential organs and so is protected, segment by segment, by little armoured plates made of a hard stuff called chitin. These plates are called tergites (on the top) and sternites (underneath).

CEPHALOTHORAX

It's that word again – the "head chest", a fusion of the head, with all its sensory organs, and the thorax, the motor room containing all the muscles used to operate the legs.

EYES

Pseudoscorpions don't have very good eyes, and some don't have any at all, relying instead on the sensory hairs on their body to tell them about their environment and prey. Most have either two or four simple, domed eyes on either side of the head.

CHELICERAE

Either side of the mouth are the pseudoscorpion's evil-looking jaws, called chelicerae. These look a bit like scissors and work like them too, slicing up and butchering prey. The chelicerae also have silk glands, which, rather surprisingly, these animals use to weave platforms and cushions used in mating and moulting.

51

Finding them...
a needle in a haystack springs to mind!

The easy way

Pseudoscorpions are everywhere. They live in compost heaps, piles of dead leaves ("leaf litter"), moss, under stones, in your house... The problem is their size and colour, which make them a challenge to spot. One cunning way to catch them is to make what's known as a **Tullgren funnel**, where a bright light is used to drive them into a jar. The principle at work here is that creatures that live in leaf litter tend to flee from light and head towards nice dark places with high humidity, where they don't have to face their deadliest enemy: dehydration.

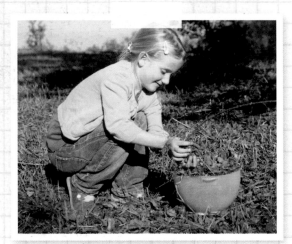

The hard way

Another technique is to scoop up a bucket of leaf litter, spread it out on a white sheet or tray, and then go through it by hand until you find your catch. It's when pseudoscorpions move that you're most likely to pick them out from among the similarly coloured litter. Their glossy appearance also helps. I found the little beast on these pages by accident when I was looking for snails under some old bricks at the bottom of my garden.

MAKING A TULLGREN FUNNEL

1. **Pack leaf litter** into a plastic funnel and wedge it in a jar, having put some damp tissue in the jar. Set a lamp over the leaves, taking care not to let the bulb touch the leaves or make them hot. (You don't want to burn the house down – the words "looking for pseudoscorpions" won't work on the insurance report!)

2. **Leave the lamp** on overnight. The next day, investigate the contents of your jar. You'll probably have an odd assortment of leaf-litter creatures such as mites, earwigs, springtails, and other stuff, but with a bit of luck you'll have a few pseudoscorpions too!

slug

How do pseudoscorpions get into your house?

Microhabitat

Because pseudoscorpions are so very tiny, you don't need a very big habitat. In fact, the biggest problem with keeping these creatures is keeping track of them. All they need to do is hunker down in the groove of a leaf and you've lost them! So I cannot stress this enough: try and make their containers as small as possible.

PSEUDOSCORPION ENCLOSURE

Catch me if you can!

Furnish the habitat with the sort of material you found your animal living in, such as bits of dead leaves. To keep the humidity up, include a pad of living moss.

An empty glitter tube makes a good home for pseudoscorpions.

Keep an eye out for runaways!

Some people have trouble keeping pseudoscorpions alive for more than a few days. The secret seems to be maintaining humidity and plentiful food. One trick to control humidity is to put plaster of Paris in the floor of the container, let it set and then moisten it before you build your habitat.

Mini-meals

Since your tiny predators feed on even tinier prey in the wild, you will have the fiddly task of supplying them with a regular supply of leaf-litter creatures, or at least a regular supply of leaf litter. Not much is known about what pseudoscorpions really like to eat, but a selection of live food including springtails and soil mites should keep your captives happy.

Springtail

Use a soft paintbrush to pick up your pseudoscorpion.

They cling to flies and hitch a ride!

MOSQUITO LARVAE

No, I haven't lost the plot and I'm not suffering from hallucinations brought on by malarial fever. And yes, I am suggesting you add these infamous bloodsuckers and spreaders of plague and pestilence to your bug zoo, and for a very good reason: mosquitoes are among the most successful and deadly animals on Earth, and it's fascinating to find out what they're really all about. You might even grow to love your pet mosquito larvae, but even if you don't, at least you'll get to know the enemy!

CREATURE FEATURES

Acquiring your stock
This couldn't be easier. Find some stagnant water in the warmer summer months – a bucket of rainwater, a water butt, a pond, even a puddle. Peer into its green shallows and you'll probably see lots of wiggly things. Just scoop some up into a jar complete with water and you're done. If you have trouble finding mosquito larvae, don't despair – just leave a bucket of water outside and it will soon get colonized.

Reflection

Water surface

SIPHON
Mosquito larvae breathe air through the siphon, which works like a clever snorkel. The end of the siphon is equipped with a water-repellent flap that opens automatically when it touches the surface and closes when the larva dives.

If your larvae lie parallel to the surface and lack siphons, they belong to a family of mosquitoes called the Anophelinae, which can spread malaria. The mosquitoes shown here belong to the Culicinae family and don't cause malaria.

Egg

Adult

Larva

The life cycle of a mosquito has four stages.

Pupa

MOSQUITO LARVA

ABDOMEN

SENSORY BRISTLES

THORAX

EYE

HEAD

ANTENNA

MOUTH BRUSH
Watch a larva for long enough and you might see a pair of fluffy brushes appear from its mouth. These are feeding combs and are wafted around to draw water into the mouth, where microscopic creatures are sieved out and swallowed.

Mosquito larvae need very little space – a tiny pot or jar will do. Their ability to thrive in tiny puddles of water is what makes mosquitoes so successful and also such a nuisance. In countries where malaria spread by mosquitoes is a big problem, people have tried getting rid of the disease by removing pools of stagnant water. The pest controllers were mystified when this didn't work, until they discovered why: old car tyres trap puddles of rainwater, and the mosquitoes were happily breeding away in them.

Moulted skins
As your little larvae grow they will moult and old skins will float to the surface. Mosquito larvae have four "instars" (larval stages) each bigger than the last.

Stagnant green water →

← Moulted skin

Larva ("wriggler") ↓

Pupa ("tumbler") ↓

Feeding
You might think that feeding such small animals would be fiddly, especially when you learn that they eat microscopic organisms like algae. How do you sort all that out? Fortunately it couldn't be easier. All that stuff is what makes stagnant water green, so all you need do is spoon stagnant green water into your micro-aquarium. For the mosquito larvae, it's like living in their own pea soup, only it's got no peas in it!

It's one of the few times that stagnant water in an aquarium is a good thing!

Tumblers
When larvae are fully grown, they turn into pupae that look like strange little prawns. This is the resting stage in the life cycle, but you wouldn't think it when you see how active they are – just jogging the jar is enough to send them twitching down into the water, only to bob back up again. This behaviour has earned them the name "tumblers". Instead of breathing through a siphon, the tumblers use "breathing trumpets" on the head. They swim by flicking a paddle on the tail.

↑ Breathing trumpet

Reflection ↑

Tumbler ↘

The tumblers have no mouths and can't eat, but you can see features of the adult insect inside, such as mouthparts, compound eyes, wings, and legs.

Paddle ▷

Taking flight
After about four days, the tumbler's skin splits and out pops a mosquito. The mosquito hangs around on the surface film to dry out and then takes off. I know what you're thinking: release these bloodsuckers and they'll come back and bite you. Well, assuming you've got *Culex pipiens* (the most common species and the one on these pages), you've little to worry about: it feeds on birds rather than humans!

Nectar: Female mosquitoes drink blood only when they're about to make eggs.

55

DRAGONFLY LARVAE

The word dragonfly conjures up images of needles of bright colour zinging and zooming over a pond in the summer sun. Unfortunately this high-energy lifestyle makes dragonflies impossible to keep in your bug zoo as adults – they'd smash themselves to bits. However, they spend most of their lives underwater as larvae, and these "baby dragons" are not only easy to keep but are every bit as exciting as their parents. Care for them well and they'll eventually reward you with one of the most breathtaking spectacles of the natural world.

PREY GRABBERS

Look close at a dragonfly larva's face and you'll see what looks like a vicious pair of jaws. This is the tip of the larva's "mask" – an extensible feeding device that unfolds to reach out and grab prey. See how it works on page 59.

CREATURE FEATURES

EYES

Huge, googly compound eyes either side of the head give these insects excellent vision.

ANTENNAE

MASK

Under the head is a hinged arm ending in powerful claws for snatching prey.

WING BUDS

On top of the animal (not visible here) are four wing buds that get bigger as the larva grows. These will eventually become the gauzy, sparkling wings of an adult dragonfly, but for now they double as supplementary gills.

THORAX

LEGS (6)

These are equipped with grappling hooks for gripping water plants.

ABDOMEN

This consists of 10 segments and contains all the breathing, breeding, and digestive gubbins.

Dragonfly skin

Keeping dragonfly larvae in your zoo is like keeping miniature crocodiles. Just like crocs, they are sly, skulking predators that hunt by lying in wait and then ambushing anything that moves. Just imagine what it would be like to scale one of these things up to the size of a 5-metre (16-foot) croc!

Land a larva

Use a fishing net (or kitchen seive fixed to a stick) to drag up a load of weed and mud from the bottom of a pond. Tip the contents of the net into a large white tray or a similar container and then, using a teaspoon, gently sort through it to look for dragonfly larvae. You'll need to concentrate: the larvae are well camouflaged and some are even covered in downy hair, making them hard to see unless they make a small movement and blow their cover!

You might find **damselfly** larvae in your sample of pond life. These look like dragonfly larvae but are more delicate, with three "tails" that are actually gills and are often flattened and leaf-like in shape. Damselfly larvae can be kept in the same way as dragonflies and make a great addition to your bug zoo.

Transfer each larva to an individual pot of water. It's important to keep them separate as they'll quite happily eat each other if crowded together, and don't collect more than two or three. Return the rest of the pond life to the pond when you've finished.

FRESHWATER AQUARIUM

A small plastic or glass aquarium is ideal for dragonfly larvae. The idea is to re-create the natural environment the larvae live in and to make it varied, so the larvae can choose where they want to be. To keep the water fresh, you will need to do at least a partial water change every week or so and remove debris such as leftover meals from the water.

Damselfly skin

1.

Put washed gravel or sand in the bottom of the tank. Gently slope the gravel so that it will make a nice backdrop and any debris will collect at the front, where it's easy to scoop out.

2.

Add pondweed, stones, and any other aquarium decorations. Heap the gravel over the roots of the plants or fix them into small pots first to keep them in place.

3.

Pop newspaper over the gravel (so the water won't mess it up) and gently pour in rainwater or tap water that's been left to stand for a few days.

4.

Leave the aquarium for at least a day to settle and clear. Position it somewhere light but not in direct sunlight.

A tea strainer makes a handy tool for moving larvae.

THE DRAGON'S DEN

Feeding time in the dragon's den is a truly exciting time and one of the highlights of your bug zoo. Once you put live prey in the tank, it won't be long before some serious predation is underway. You can even tease your dragonfly into striking with its mask by holding prey in front of it with homemade wooden tweezers.

Some dragonfly larvae can extend and withdraw their masks to capture prey in less than 15 milliseconds. That's faster than the human eye can register!

Feeding
Dragonfly larvae need a constant supply of fresh – and that means living – food. Anything that will wriggle and move in the water will catch your larva's huge eyes, but you'll need to experiment to see what size prey it wants to tackle. Small larvae might prefer tiny prey such as water fleas or mosquito larvae. For bigger ones, bloodworms (common in ponds), earthworms, and fish fry are tackled with gusto.

FEEDING TIME

Larva coming in for the kill

Mealworm

Tweezer

You can tease your larva into striking by dangling wriggling prey near it or even by shining a light spot with an LED torch. To hold the prey, use chopsticks or make wooden tweezers from kebab sticks. To make the tweezers, wrap an elastic band around one stick to form a pivot and another elastic band around the "handles" to make the long ends springy.

Collecting exuviae

You might be alarmed one day to find what looks like a dead larva on the surface of the water in your tank. More often than not this is just the empty skin, or "exuviae", left behind when a dragonfly or damselfly larva moults – something that happens many times as they grow up. Look in the water and you'll find a bigger larva (perhaps 25 per cent bigger) looking a little pale and vulnerable as he waits for his new skin to harden up. The empty skins can be collected and dried. Try sticking them on a piece of card with the dates of the moults and you'll get a nice little growth chart of your pet's progress.

Feeding mask

Hinge

If your exuviae is dry and crispy, soak it in water to make it flexible again. Then use a pin to pull out the mask. This is a great way of getting to know your larva without causing the living animal any stress.

I'm outta here!

WATER TO WINGS

Place sticks in the tank so the larva can climb out for its final moult.

The breathtaking finale of your larva's life is its transformation into an adult dragonfly or damselfly. It's a true miracle and something everyone should see at least once in their life. Predicting it can be tricky, but there are clues. The larva's wing buds will flesh out and its eyes will look vacant. It will go off food and start to hang around the surface as its gills stop working. Make sure there are sticks that it can climb up to leave the water. When the time comes, the larva will climb one of these, hunch up, and its skin will split open. Very slowly, a ghostly pale and very crumpled dragonfly will almost ooze out. It's moments like this that digital cameras were made for! Watch the wings inflate and the body colour up and harden. Finally, it will beat its sparkling wings and take off.

It's time to say goodbye and open a door or window to let your captive fly free!

Once my wings have dried I'll be off!

WATER BOATMEN

The water boatman is a ferocious underwater predator found in ponds, lakes, and streams. It reminds me in some ways of a bird of prey, but instead of surveying the land from high above, it hangs upside-down from the water surface to watch the watery world below. And when it spots victims with its huge eyes, it swoops down and plucks them from the pondweed before returning to its perch to devour them. Its active lifestyle makes this bug-eyed monster a very entertaining addition to your zoo.

CREATURE FEATURES

Water surface

Reflection of water boatman

All this hanging around has given me a headache!

FRONT LEGS

The first two pairs of legs are tipped with claws for grasping prey.

REAR LEGS

The rear legs are fringed with fine hairs and are used like oars to row the insect through the water.

ROSTRUM OR BEAK

This is a sharp and flexible feeding tube used to stab prey and inject a toxic saliva, which subdues and digests the victim. The rostrum is then used like a drinking straw to suck up the victim's body fluids.

HEAD

COMPOUND EYES

The enormous compound eyes, each made of hundreds of tiny eyes, look like mean wraparound shades or a sci-fi space helmet. Like the eyes of dragonflies, which are similar, they form very good images and are used to locate prey. They are also sensitive to polarized light (more about that later).

Built like a boat

The water boatman not only has "oars" for propelling itself but has a body shaped like the hull of a rowing boat – perfect for slipping easily through the water. Because it swims upside down on its back, it's also known as a "backswimmer".

THORAX

ABDOMEN

WAXY HAIRS
A layer of waxy, water-repellent hairs covers the abdomen. Water boatmen trap a film of air under the hair and around the body.

AIR BUBBLE
Although water boatmen live in water, they breathe air. They trap a silvery film of air around the body and under the wings, enclosing themselves in a kind of bubble. They use this bubble to breathe and to control their buoyancy.

AIR HOLE
When the tip of the abdomen touches the water surface, the waxy hairs around it spread out and an air hole opens up. This allows the insect to replenish its air supply. The hairs close over the hole automatically when the animal dives.

WINGS
It might surprise you to learn that water boatmen can fly! Their flight wings are protected under leathery wing cases. Air trapped under them gives the wings a silvery appearance in water.

THE BOATHOUSE

Mealworm

Water boatmen need a freshwater home made in the same way as the dragonfly aquarium on page 57. They don't need a huge tank – a large jar or fish bowl will do. As they are carnivorous, it's not a good idea to crowd them, keep youngsters with adults, or put other creatures with them (except for live prey). A big jar like the one below will comfortably house 2–3 adults.

Finding them

Pond, lakes, and slow-moving streams are good places to look. Approach slowly and have a careful look – they will appear to be hanging from the surface. Even if they dive down, disturbed by your approach, they will bob back up. Use a net or a sieve on a stick to scoop them out. Be quick and have a bucket or tray of water on standby for your captives as they will immediately start hopping and jumping around to try and escape.

Close relatives

Lesser water boatman

Water boatmen make up a family of insects known as Notonectidae. You might also come across smaller but similar-looking insects called lesser water boatmen (family Corixidae), which swim the right way up and stay near the bottom, where they feed on plants. Although not as big and spectacular as notonectids, they are quite cool and even sing to each other, making a rasping noise by rubbing their legs on their heads!

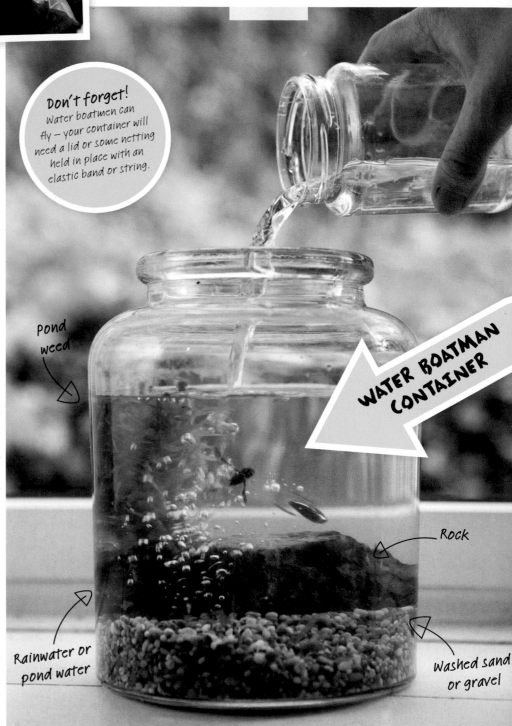

Don't forget!
Water boatmen can fly – your container will need a lid or some netting held in place with an elastic band or string.

pond weed

WATER BOATMAN CONTAINER

Rock

Rainwater or pond water

Washed sand or gravel

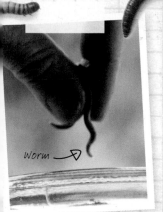

Worm →

🍽 Feeding

Water boatmen only take live and wriggling prey. Mine eat everything from small worms and mealworms (available in pet shops) to fly maggots (from fishing shops), flies, and tadpoles. You can also put small pond creatures in with them as this is what they'd eat in the wild. As soon as the prey is in the water, watch the hunt. Besides using their eyes to see prey, water boatmen have sensory hairs on their legs and abdomen that allow them to feel the movements of live prey and so capture them in dark or murky water.

THINGS TO LOOK OUT FOR

When they attack prey, you will be able to watch the grisly feeding process in detail. First the water boatman stabs its victim with its highly mobile and flexible beak. Then, when the prey is paralysed or dead, you'll see the killer start sucking out the body fluids. I've watched one devour a tadpole this way, the tadpole's body slowly deflating like a balloon over an hour or so.

✋ Sunny side up

You can demonstrate exactly what it is that makes a boatman swim upside down by putting one in a clear container of water and, in a dark room, lighting the insect from below with a torch – it will flip up the right way round!

Grooming time
Like many predators from peregrine falcons to your pet cat, water boatmen are fastidious in their vanity. They will spend a lot of time grooming, rubbing their eyes, wings, and waterproof hair with their legs.

✋ Boatman to aeronaut in seconds

Water boatmen are often the first creatures to colonize a new pond – but how? Well, you can see for yourself. Taking care not to get bitten, remove one from the water, hold it in the flat of your hand and let it dry out. This may take a few minutes, and they do have a tendency to flip around to try and hop back into the water – so be prepared to juggle it.

After a while, when the insect realizes it's not going to flip itself back into the water, it will give up this tactic and fall back on another mode of locomotion. Watch it carefully as it wipes its eyes and back with its legs – this is the boatman's pre-flight check. Soon after it will "unclip" its wings and spread them before suddenly springing into the air and buzzing off!

Yes, they are excellent flyers and once they're up in the air will search for a new pond, river, or lake by looking for the polarized light that these natural surfaces reflect. The problem is that glass buildings and car windscreens also reflect polarized light, which means that water boatmen can make mistakes. Sit in a car park on a hot and sunny day and you'll sometimes see water boatmen and other pond insects such as water beetles come crashing down!

INDEX

Useful websites and further information

AES Bug Club (amentsoc.org/bug-club) – Just about the only UK club for younger people (age 5–15) into invertebrates.

Alana Ecology (alanaecology.com) – A supplier of all manner of equipment for the zoo keeper, from pots and tweezers to nets and cages.

Anglian Lepidopterists Supplies (angleps.btinternet.co.uk) – A supplier of everything for the bug hunter young or old. Including cages, pots and nets.

British Dragonfly Society (dragonflysoc.org.uk) – If dragonflies make you buzz and you want to know more, try this website.

Buglife (buglife.org.uk) – The invertebrate conservation trust; lots of creepy crawly related stuff on their website.

Butterfly Conservation (butterfly-conservation.org) – An organisation dedicated to conserving butterflies and moths. They also have good stuff for younger enthusiasts on their website

Dino-lite (absolute-data-services.co.uk) – High quality digital USB microscope specialists.

Virginia Cheeseman (virginiacheeseman.co.uk) – If you want to get all exotic (I'm thinking stick insects and tarantulas), then Virginia is worth checking out.

Wildlife Watch (wildlifewatch.org.uk) – The younger membership of the UK Wildlife Trusts partnership. There are local wildlife trusts throughout the UK, which means there will be one near you. A good place to get questions answered and find out more about insects and other wildlife.

Nick Baker would like to thank James at Absolute Data Services for loan of the Dino-lite microscope, and Andy at Alana Ecology.

Dorling Kindersley would like to thank Scarlet Heap and Stanley Heap for appearing in photographs, and Ceri Baker for her lovely lunches on photoshoots. The publisher would also like to thank the following for their kind permission to reproduce their photographs. (Key: a-above; b-below/bottom; c-centre; f-far; l-left; r-right; t-top)

Alamy Images: Arco Images GmbH / H. Frei 56tl; Lee Beel 27bc; Blickwinkel / Hecker 33bc; Blickwinkel / Kottmann 53bc; Blickwinkel / MeulvanCauteren 32clb; Nigel Cattlin 21ca; Matt Cole 11tr; Graphic Science 21clb, 35tr; David J. Green - animals 13ca; Chris Howes / Wild Places 49fclb; Hazel Jeffs 59bc; Lars S. Madsen 62fclb; Mercer / Insects 56; Nature Picture Library / Jose B. Ruiz 44bc; Robert Pickett / Papilio 11cra; Stefan Sollfors 43tc; Barry Turner 36bl; WildPictures 18tl. **Ardea:** Johan de Meester 25fcr; Steve Hopkin 36clb, 41fcra; David Spears (Last Refuge) 10br. **Corbis:** Naturfoto Honal / Klaus Honal 59fbr, 59fcr, 59fcra, 59fcrb, 59ftr; Hans Pfletschinger / Science Faction 41cl; Fritz Rauschenbach 47cla; Stefan Sollfors / Science Faction 45bc, 45clb; Visuals Unlimited 21cb, 29tr, 47ftr; Stuart Westmorland 14cl. **Dorling Kindersley:** Natural History Museum, London 6cl, 22fclb; Oxford Scientific Films 37br, 41ftl; Jerry Young 6crb, 11ftl. **Flickr.com:** Michael Balke 29crb; Rodents Rule / Carron Brown 17fcra; Captain Spaulding78 / Tim 11tc. **FLPA:** Nigel Cattlin 11cr, 11crb; Imagebroker 46-47; Imagebroker / Andre Skonieczny, I 36r; Mitsuhiko Imamori / Minden Pictures 10tr; Roger Tidman 47fcra. **Getty Images:** Botanica / Steve Satushek 19tl; Flickr / Achim Mittler, Frankfurt am Main 36bc, 40cr; National Geographic / Wolcott Henry 10clb; Panoramic Images 43ftr; Photographer's Choice / Derek Croucher 36cl; Photographer's Choice / Guy Edwardes 27cb; Photographer's Choice / Sami Sarkis 63crb; Photolibrary / Colin Milkins 20b; Photolibrary / Oxford Scientific 41tc; Stock Image / Stephen Swain Photography 16tl; Stone / Peter J. Bryant / BPS 22-23cb; Stone / NHMPL 21cla; Workbook Stock / Steve Satushek 47cr. **Krister Hall:** Photo.net 11br. **iStockphoto.com:** Alexander Hafemann 4 (blank page); Tomasz Kopalski 17crb; Alexander Kuzovlev 7fcra (snail), 15bl, 64tr; Dave Lewis 17cr, 17ftr; Trevor Nielson 11bl (35mm frame), 17ca (35mm frame); Bill Noll 53tr; Tomasz Zachariasz 11fcr, 12tr. **Thomas Marent:** 6-7t (butterfly), 26bl, 26cl, 26fbl, 26fcl, 26tc, 27br, 27cla; naturepl.com: Philippe Clement 29cra. **Photolibrary:** Oxford Scientific (OSF) 28crb; Oxford Scientific (OSF) / David M Dennis 49cr. **Photoshot:** NHPA / A.N.T. Photo Library 49fbl; NHPA / George Bernard 55crb; NHPA / Laurie Campbell 10fclb. **Science Photo Library:** Dr. Jeremy Burgess 40cl; Claude Nuridsany & Marie Perennou 40bl, 40br, 41bl; Andrew Syred 40ftl.

All other images © Dorling Kindersley
For further information see: www.dkimages.com

Yum, dinner